FRUIT IN FAILURE

Tales from Mountains I Never Climbed

ADAM G. COOPER

Copyright © 2023 by Adam G. Cooper
All rights reserved. This book may not be
reproduced, in whole or in part, in any form, without
written permission from the author.
Published by Energeia Press, Melbourne, 2023

My eyes turn upward to the looming peaks.
"My God!" I gasp. "How will I ever survive this?"

Songs of King David
Circa. 970 B.C.E.

Cover photo: On the icefields near Mueller Hut, Mount Cook Region, New Zealand. Photo on page 60 kindly provided by the Federation Quebecoise de la Montagne et de l'Escalade. Photo on page 114 reproduced with kind permission from Lorne Gill at Nature Scot. All other photos are from the author's own collection.

CONTENTS

Chapter 1	Failing Well	3
Chapter 2	Beneath Kibo	11
Chapter 3	Superstar at Arapiles	23
Chapter 4	The Outdoor Athlete	29
Chapter 5	Abseil Fail at the Onkas	37
Chapter 6	Channel Nine at Morialta	43
Chapter 7	Avalanched on Mt Cook	49
Chapter 8	Thin Ice in the Rockies	55
Chapter 9	The Wolf	61
Chapter 10	Mt Andromeda Fail	65
Chapter 11	Death on Alpamayo	69
Chapter 12	The Mountain Lion	73
Chapter 13	Terrorists in Huaraz	83
Chapter 14	Tragic Deaths	91
Chapter 15	Diamond Couloir Fail	95
Chapter 16	Fall on Centre Post Direct	103
Chapter 17	No Picnic on Mont Blanc: I	115
Chapter 18	No Picnic on Mont Blanc: II	127
Chapter 19	No Picnic on Mont Blanc: III	139
Chapter 20	Burglar in Langtang	151
Chapter 21	The Need for Speed	163
Chapter 22	Blown off Mt Buller	175
Chapter 23	Epilogue	187

The author geared up to ski the Vallée Blanche, French Alps, 2013.

CHAPTER ONE

FAILING WELL

I am a very ordinary climber. My achievements on rock, ice, and alpine routes do not rate a mention in any esteemed climbing circles. I have never climbed Everest, never entered the "death-zone", never pioneered any significant new routes. I have no heroic example to hold out to budding climbers who want to reach for the stars and fulfil their dreams, for I have been to the highest summits of exactly zero countries and continents on earth.

Sometimes I have tried to make excuses for my failure as a mountaineer. For a start, my physique is not well suited for hard rock climbing. While at six foot six I may have great reach, I am also heavy, and weigh in at a lean 110 kg. I'd have done alright as a rugby winger, but burn out quickly on an overhang. I also have a few congenital and chronic ailments. I was born with spina bifida occulta in the lumbar spine, and have taken digoxin, beta blockers, and aspirin for a heart defect since it was diagnosed at the age of 25. I have chronic nerve and circulation problems in my feet. I sweat profusely and so easily get wet and chilled. My boots are always too tight, my gloves too small, my sleeping bag too short. And so on.

But then I read stories about the climbing achievements of people with severe physical disabilities. Over fifteen disabled climbers have summited Everest, including several double amputees! By contrast, I have always been healthy, active, and athletically able. Neither a lengthy anatomy nor a dodgy heart prevent a person from exercising the truly non-negotiable practices necessary for athletic excellence: mental resilience, sound judgement, and sheer dogged determination.

So what is this book about? Well, as the title suggests, it is not a catalogue of remarkable climbing achievements. It is, rather, a litany of climbing failures. It is an autobiographical collection of humiliating tales of defeat, embarrassing stories about mountains I have never successfully climbed, goals I have never reached, best laid schemes that have "gang aft agley." In that sense this book is something like a project in solidarity with the vast sea of average Jill and Joes who will never climb like a Catherine Destivelle or a Lyn Hill, an Alex Honnold or a Ueli Steck, yet who can't help but feel something of the same yearning, enchantment, and motivation which only the actual experience of climbing and standing among great alpine ranges can inspire. You know your limits, whether in ability or opportunity. But you have also felt the captivating call presented to you in climbing to test your known limits, to extend yourself, to find and realize your purpose and meaning in life in an *ekstasis* (a standing outside yourself), as the ancient philosophers would say.

There is a well-known adage among climbers: you're only as good as your next climb. It expresses a commonly felt anticlimactic feeling every climber has after a noteworthy personal success on a route. You should be feeling elated. You should be feeling proud, grateful, satisfied. Your family and friends think that you should now be over whatever it was that drove you to such lengths, that you should have it out of your system, that you can get on with life in the "real world" at last. Instead you feel empty, eaten up inside by a curious and unfathomable melancholy, a reconstituting and insatiable hunger for more: something steeper, longer, harder, colder, more isolated, or, best of all, unclimbed. It is only when I have fulfilled that urge, grasped hold of the new challenge taking shape inside me, before me, that I will be happy, that I will be "over it." But of course, I never reach that goal. It's like making love. You are sure that this time it will make all things right, this time will be better than the last. But after all the huffing and puffing, after all the playful or animal exuberance, after all the expressions of affection and satisfaction, you are overwhelmed with a melancholic spirit, liquefied by the *petit mort*, reduced back down to your carnal, finite self. You become aware that despite the wonder and grace of it all, there is more:

more to this relationship, more to happiness, more to life. There is always more. Our true fulfilment lies in a beyond.

In a line that inspired the title of this book, American alpinist Steve House once remarked how deceptive success in the mountains can be. "Failure is the more valuable fruit, borne as it is from the knurled vine of process. Taking up crampons and ice axes after failure forces me to own my own shortcomings, learn from them, and to capitalize on the strengths that I have found."[1] Many climbing coaches, along with a growing school of researchers, are now referring to the value of failure, regarding it as a potentially positive experience in one's overall approach to and assessment of progress. House and others call this approach "learning to fail well," or "intelligent failure." The adage about only being as good as the next climb expresses a personal re-evaluation, a necessary relativization of my best effort. Perhaps I did do well. Perhaps it was a laudable or even superlative achievement, comparatively speaking. But now that it is done, none of that matters. There is only what lies ahead. No matter how poorly or well you climb, no matter how mediocre or outstanding your gym, crag or alpine achievements, it's actually a level playing field. If it is true that you are only as good as your next climb, if *all* climbers are only as good as their next climb, then the field lies

---

[1] Steve House, *Beyond the Mountain* (Sheffield: Vertebrate Publishing, 2010), 173.

open, and every attempt to rate yourself according to your past accomplishments is misguided.

I understand that not every person interested in reading this book will be a dedicated climber. I don't believe you have to be to enjoy it. Although I have always appreciated Yvon Chouinard's assessment of adventure travel as "pure bullshit," there is possibly enough travel and adventure in these tales to arouse interest in this world's natural wonders and to enable a certain imaginative escape to environments beyond the immediate and familiar. There may also be some historical value in the tales about certain personages and the accounts of traditional climbing in South Australia in the 1980s. As far as I know, the Channel Nine visit to Morialta in the 1990s has not been recounted elsewhere, and the Glenelg beach bouldering wall has long since been demolished.

Of course, not all my climbs were fails. My mountaineering exploits have taken me to six continents, and I have told here of some successful ascents, and of the redeeming qualities possessed by those that weren't. The quality of a climbing adventure lies in aspects that cannot be reduced to success or failure in sending the route or reaching the summit. Moreover, many tales have been left out. I have not included stories about my deportation from Argentina, the tarantula in the Santa Cruz Valley, the lynx attack on a young chamoix in Argentière, rock fall strike beneath Malte Brun (with a hole in my pack to this day as witness), exploring prayer-caves in the crags of northern Iraq, winter-soloing Scotland's Buachaille Etiv Mor, ice-cragging in the English Pennines, lightning strike in Westland, New Year's Eve midnight solo of Cascade Falls, and so on. In a time of my life where I have faced unprecedented personal challenges, recounting what I have here has provided an unexpected recovery of self. As I entered my thirties and forties, my climbing experiences defined me less and less while family, vocational and academic endeavours increasingly occupied the centre. Looking back through these relived memories I can now see that my early years of climbing shaped me more than I knew. It was not just I who went into the mountains. They went into me, into my bones and soul and blood, mysteriously contributing to my entire self-constitution. With the reflection that has been prompted by writing these stories, I can finally acknowledge that, despite all the summits never reached, I really have had some extraordinary mountain adventures. I should stop lamenting my dashed or abandoned dreams and just get on with it: with climbing, with training, with life, and last but not least, with this book.

Mt Cook viewed from the south, 1987.

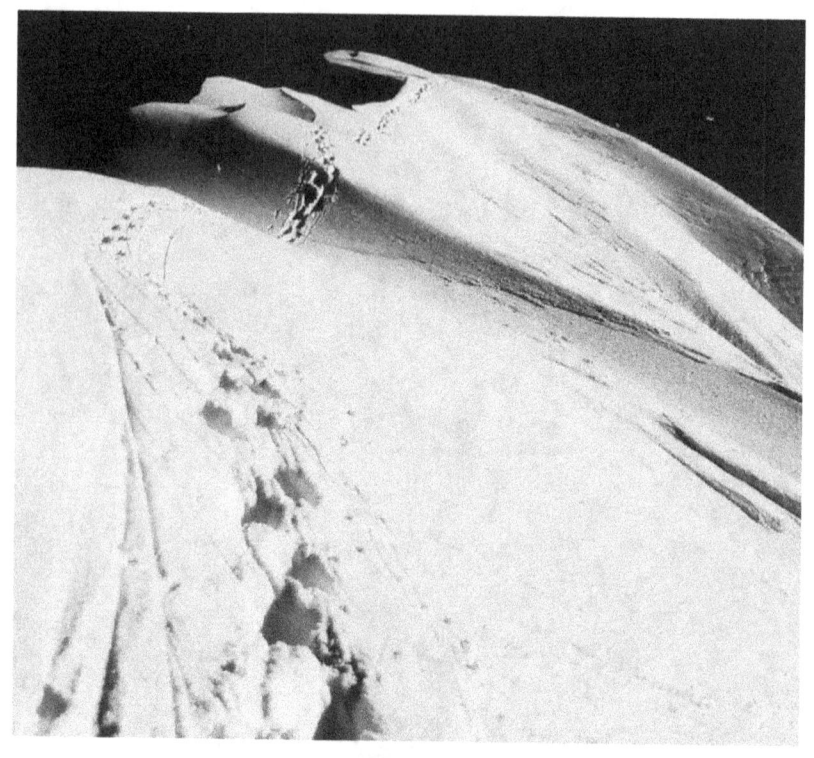

Summit ridge of Nevado Pisco (5752m), Peru.

CHAPTER TWO
BENEATH KIBO

My earliest memories of wanting to climb stem from my childhood years living at the foot of Mt Kilimanjaro in Tanzania. It was the mid-1970s. My father was a teacher at the international school in Moshi, and my mother nursing my baby brother, just-born youngest of four boys. Our family's small bungalow, surrounded by mango trees, was set in the midst of maize and coffee fields, and lay in direct view of Kibo's soaring white summit and Mawenzi's rugged crags. The river that ran alongside our place, where we would explore after school and look for Colobus monkeys, was fed from its snows. I remember sitting oftentimes in the branches of the jacaranda tree outside our shared bedroom window, gazing longingly at the white glaciers of the upper slopes of Kibo, rent by the vast Breach Wall, mesmerized by hopes of savouring for myself those inaccessible wonders.

It was no wonder then that I suffered such bitter disappointment one day when I learned that my two older brothers, and not I, had been invited on a school trek up to Horombo Hut on the now nicknamed "Coca-Cola" route on Kilimanjaro above Marangu. I couldn't believe the injustice of it. Despite my pleading and desperate defence of my ability to keep up, at six years old I was considered too young for the altitude, and on the night following their departure to the mountain with my father I cried myself to sleep.

We returned to Australia in 1976, and although no opportunity to climb presented itself in the years ahead, my childhood in mostly rural settings was filled with mischievous adventure. I took to hiking, hunting, rabbit trapping, and fishing, either with my brothers or alone. I avidly consumed climbing literature, studied maps, planned expeditions, and created lengthy equipment lists. My dream in life was to return to Moshi to work as a doctor at KCMC, the Kilimanjaro Christian Medical Centre. This was the ill-equipped hospital where Rob Taylor underwent treatment (and torture) after his leg-shattering fall while climbing the icicle of the Breach Wall with Henry Barber in 1978.[2] From there I felt I could simultaneously serve the world and embrace adventure. But although I did well enough at school, I was prone to distraction and keeping bad company, and my parents must have feared greatly for my future when at eight I was

---

[2] See Rob Taylor's personal account of events in *The Breach: Kilimanjaro and the Conquest of Self* (1981).

arrested for arson (accidental) and at twelve got away with a police warning for vandalism (also accidental, kind of...).

I was sixteen years old and in my final year of school in Adelaide when I finally started climbing. I had got a part time job at one of Adelaide's outdoor shops and saved enough to pay for a six-week indoor climbing course at the Parks Community Centre. The wall there was unlike today's climbing walls with their bolt-on molded holds. It was instead built of brick and creatively reproduced a wide range of real-life crag features. The sessions ran on Friday nights and for the first meeting I had to catch several buses to get there. From then on however I was offered a ride to and fro' by one of the other course participants, a dope-smoking builder whose old Kingswood smelled like an opium den.

After the six weeks the course culminated in a two-day outdoor climbing experience at Morialta Falls. By this time I had purchased my own gear for top roping, but as a school boy whose only friends thought I was mad I found it hard to find a climbing partner. That didn't stop me from abseiling, and I abseiled off nearly everything I could find, which included not only all the obvious cliffs at Morialta but also oddities like the crumbling and overhanging Black Cliff at Hallett Cove and the smooth granite Reedy Creek cliffs near Palmer. I also taught myself to solo top-rope belay, using a petzl jumar on an 11mm static rope. Having got my driver's licence soon after I turned sixteen, I was able to borrow my parents' car most weekends, and when I couldn't, rode my bike from the western suburbs all the way up Norton Summit Road instead. On my final day of matriculation in 1985, on so-called muck-up day, I planned to abseil off the Immanuel College Chapel, and had even found a way through the man-hole onto the roof. But I lacked tactical support from my peers and chickened out on the day, perhaps an early sign of my perennial tendency to play it safe rather than push through the risks.

At the beginning of 1986, as I turned seventeen, I started planning my first New Zealand alpine climbing trip. I had done a solo walk in south-west Tasmania during the September school holidays the year before, and despite getting wet, cold, and disoriented on Mt Olympus, was eager to seek out bigger hills. I wrote to Dave Macleod from Alpine Guides Westland, and Dave agreed to take me on a specially arranged course up the Fox Glacier in September, though he had never had someone as young as me before, and demanded that I get fit. So I started running, and when I couldn't climb I went bouldering at the Norton Summit cave by lamplight at night, or along the long stone wall that used to border the lawns at the Glenelg beach foreshore. The cave was sheltered from the rain in winter, while the wall was particularly attractive in summer, as I could ride my bike down to Glenelg in the evenings, boulder on the wall for an hour, then cool off with a swim before heading home.

It was at the Glenelg wall that I met Simon Parsons, legendary hardman of Tasmanian rock, who was completing his medical degree in Adelaide. Simon was all athlete and playful energy and, although nearly ten years my senior, very friendly towards me. He took me along in his classic Saab 900 turbo to belay and photograph him doing hard climbs at Norton Summit and Victor Harbor, some of which I published with an article on South Australian rock climbing in *Action Outdoor* magazine. At a later time I met up with Simon again at Arapiles, and watched in amazement as he led classic test-pieces like *India* (29) and *Have a Good Flight Direct* (27). He possessed beautiful form when climbing, and I have always tried to imitate his precision, poise, elegance and balance on rock, though with nothing like his strength and courage. With his encouragement I led *Little Thor* (20), and later *Pilot Error* (21) and *The British Beat* (21), to date my best climbs on rock. His stories of climbing hard rock with Kim Carrigan and steep ice with John Fantini fueled my imagination and motivation. My favourite memory of Simon is blasting along the road in his Saab from Arapiles to Horsham at 170 kph, windows down and Sade's seductive voice issuing smoothly from the stereo through the wind. Having owned and tuned classic Saab turbos in my middle age, including the incomparable c900, I know now for myself the thrill of their sharp torque curve and driver-focused dash design.

September soon came and I headed off for New Zealand, hitch-hiking my way from Christchurch to Fox Glacier township via Arthur's Pass. Dave had found one other client to share the course, and the three of us flew by helicopter into Fox Glacier hut, perched just above the icefall, with six days' supplies. It was my first time in glaciated terrain and I was enchanted by the creaks, crashes, and groans of the ice-fall, the rumble of avalanches, and the towering white spires surrounding us. The course taught us crampon technique, ice axe arrest, crevasse rescue, avalanche safety and rescue, snow belays, snow survival, and numerous snow and ice climbing and rope work skills. The September conditions made for slow going, as we waded around the nearby valleys, gullies, ridges, and plateaus through deep spring snow. But it was the perfect initiation for me and my new-found love for rock-climbing found its happy complement in this alpine version of the extraordinary pursuit.

With our week above Fox Glacier concluded, I hitch-hiked down to Wanaka for a few days, learning to ski for the first time. Then I hitched to Mt Cook village where I teamed up with a pair of Canadian skiers (one of whom - Jim Baker, now of Banff Mountain Film Festival fame - became a climbing colleague and long-term friend) for a multi-day ski touring trip up the Tasman Glacier. I was a novice on skis, but I had a rope and my newly learned glacial travel technique to share. After catching a back-flight in via ski-plane, I struggled at first to ski with a pack on, and fell often in the steeper snow fields around Tasman Saddle Hut where we were based. I felt embarrassed by my ineptitude, and watched on enviously as the two Canadians carved up the slopes below Hochstetter Dome on their telemark skis with easy virtuosity. By the time we skied out five days later via Beetham Valley, however, I had gained enough proficiency to make sweeping turns on easier angled slopes. In bidding my Canadian friends farewell, I made arrangements for Jim to meet me at Arapiles that summer, floating tentative plans of a future climbing trip to his hometown in Banff, smack-bang in the heart of the Canadian Rockies.

I made that trip to Canada at the end of the next year, 1987, stopping first for two months in New Zealand again. By then I had gained the experience of living like a true climbing drop-out at Arapiles for weeks on end, meeting legends like HB (Malcolm Matheson), Louise Shepherd, Jon Muir and Greg Child. I never climbed hard, and in fact accomplished very little, due partly to my innate lack of courage (animated by too active an imagination of what would happen if I fell), and partly to my failure to secure a climbing partner. Besides the rendezvous with Jim and other occasionally passing pilgrims, I often found myself partnerless at the Pines. During those days I would usually spend the cooler mornings bouldering and doing pullups, and the afternoons brewing tea, reading the guidebook, sorting gear, and snoozing, and through it all basically trying to look and feel like a real climber who belonged in the place.

On one occasion my fortunes changed when a Swiss couple set up camp alongside me. He looked like a serious climber fresh out of some European movie: lean, brown, strong, and tall, with long blond hair and bright blue eyes. His wife was also athletic, but was sporting a prominent baby bump. She was obviously heavily pregnant. On the morning after their arrival, the Swiss superman approached my tent with his climbing pack on, looking ready for a day out. Maybe this was the moment I had been waiting for. A real partner at last. A climbing superstar who would lend me his courage and brawn, while I could belay like no one else, and could personally guide him around all the crags and climbs, which I knew (from the guidebook!) like the back of my hand.

"Hey, how's it going?" he called as he approached my tent. "I was just wondering if you have any climbing planned for today?"

I trembled inside with anticipation. This was it. This was my open door to a new world, a new future. "Ahh, I'd love to. I've been looking for someone to climb with for days. What about you?"

"Actually I've already got plans to climb with another guy for the next two weeks, but I was wondering if you wanted to climb with my wife? She's six months pregnant, so she can't climb anything too difficult, but she'd really like to get out and do something."

And so my destiny was realized. I was to climb with this neighbourly woman-with-child. But as it turned out, how fitting a destiny it was. Anna may have been heavily pregnant, but she was lithe, strong, and fit. We settled on *Arachnus*, the classic four pitch grade 9 on the Watchtower Face. With shared leads, she proved more than the partner I needed, and her amiable company and confidence-inspiring style made my day.

There was one tiny crisis that nearly eventuated, and that could have ruined the day. While she was leading the first pitch, and I was sat on a rock at the base belaying, a large brown snake slithered into view. It was sliding along the base of the cliff towards me, where the rock meets the ground. At that moment, Anna was stationary, either putting in protection or perhaps working out a tricky section. Either way, she was out of sight. I froze when I saw the snake, but as it slithered closer, I nervously began to wonder what to do. If Anna moved or called for rope, I would have to move too. But then the snake might strike. I had to do something, before it got too close. When it was only a few feet away from me, I deliberately startled it, shifting my feet and issuing a sharp hissing sound. The snake stopped and reared back and up, its head swaying in the air and its tongue flickering with agitation. Then it darted away, back the way it had come, just as the rope pulled upwards and I had to pay out slack.

How laughable that my most terrifying moment as a wanna-be prospective career climber should have arisen in the form of a snake, as it did for the first man in his paradise. And that while enjoying one of my most memorable days out, with the delightful Anna, six months pregnant, from Switzerland. It was our only climb together. The next day she and her husband packed up shop and moved to Horsham, to be nearer more comfortable amenities. I too soon packed up. Having run out of money, I needed to get back to work at the outdoor shop, and save my pennies again for my grand New Zealand and Canada expedition. And so ended another of my numerous half-baked adventures at the Piles.

The author leading *The British Beat* (21), Mt Arapiles (1989).

Following on *Cassandra* (18), Mt Arapiles (1989).

Keith "Noddy" Lockwood, 2020.

CHAPTER THREE

SUPERSTAR AT ARAPILES

After a decade or more of absence, recent years have seen a resurgence in my climbing visits to Arapiles. I have been blessed to get to know and climb with Keith "Noddy" Lockwood, whose theologian brothers I have known well through my own vocational circles since the early 1990s. Keith continues to surprise by still leading exploratory adventures up virgin lines. He has demonstrated to me that the days of pioneering quality new 'trad' routes at Arapiles are far from over.

Conversations with Keith have ranged in focus from accounts of his early days mountaineering in New Zealand and Patagonia to incidents with famous climbers he has known. Rockfall on the Sheila face, new routes in the Darrans, uncrossed passes in northern Patagonia: his overseas climbing accomplishments, largely unsung, impress me as much as his endless list of creme de la creme new routes in Australia since the 1970s, not to mention his literary achievements and tireless championing of an environmentally responsible rock-climbing culture.

One story Keith related to me concerned the visit to Arapiles in 1988 of David Lee Roth, one time lead singer of the rock band Van Halen. Surprisingly the visit passed by relatively unnoticed, receiving only local media attention. Keith, who at the time was a journalist at the Wimmera Mail Times, received a tip-off about the arrival of Roth's huge entourage at the Mount. Neither the name David Lee Roth nor Van Halen meant anything to Nod, a true country rustic. But he headed out to the Mount nonetheless to see what all the fuss was about and whether he could come up with a worthwhile story. On ambling up to the Plaque area, he happened upon what seemed to be a mini travelling circus: two tour buses were parked in the blazing sun, plus three or four vehicles, surrounded by tent shade awnings, umbrellas, folding chairs, and oodles of people milling about. On the Plaque cliff a number of top ropes were strung up, with much attention focused on a strapping young man with a reversed base-ball cap puffing on a top-rope about half-way up Maximus (17). Nod whipped around to the top and, leaning over the lip with his camera, managed to squeeze off a few nice shots of the rock-star just past the crux.

While Roth forced a smile for the camera, according to Nod's version of events, it turned out Roth wasn't too happy to have had some unauthorized photos taken, though later calmed down when he learned they were destined only for the local country newspaper. One picture did go further, ending up in Keith's superlative study *Arapiles: A Million Mountains* (2007). It is hard to tell if the yawning grimace on Roth's face is one of terror or delight!

Keith's account of Roth's visit interested me all the more in that I have my own story to tell about the rockstar's visit to Arapiles. Earlier in the same year, I had caught up with an American lass at Arapiles whom I had met in New Zealand the year before. In New Zealand we had exchanged contact details and agreed to meet up at Arapiles to do some climbing for a few days. Debbie and I climbed mostly in the Organ Pipes, and she was impressed by Arapiles' quartz-hard bulging sandstone and varied terrain. On parting she promised to be back.

A couple of months' later I was woken by a phone-call in the dead of night. Nobody ever called us at this hour. I was 20 at the time, still living at home, and I heard my mother answering the phone in her serious formal voice, no doubt fearing some bad news about a death in the family. But then the tone of her voice changed to her polite, motherly, caring voice, and she put down the receiver and padded towards my room. "It's for you dear," she said softly, "a young lady calling from America."

America? Who could it be, I wondered, as I stumbled to the phone and held the receiver up to my ear. My voice was broken and croaky. "Hello?"

"Hey Adam, remember me? It's Debbie calling from the U.S.!" she shouted enthusiastically. "How's the climbing?" The words entered my ears but meant nothing. It took me some moments to piece things together in my mind. Debbie? The U.S.? Oh yes, Debbie, Arapiles, rock climbing, New Zealand. In the background I could hear loud banging music and raucous voices. Still in stupor I mumbled some kind of idiotic reply, disoriented and half-asleep. She ploughed on undaunted. "Hey, guess what? David Lee Roth is coming to Australia, and he wants to go rock climbing with you at Arapiles!"

"David who?"

"David Lee Roth, the rock star! The lead singer from Van Halen! He's right here with me at a party in Seattle, and he wants to go climbing at Arapiles!"

I had heard of Van Halen – my brothers' musical interests ensured that much - but the name David Lee Roth meant nothing at that dread hour and I failed entirely to fire to the keen spark of her excitement. "Umm, yeah ok. That sounds great. Look, um, it's two o'clock in the morning here, so um, maybe could you call back during the day sometime and we can work something out? Or maybe write me a letter."

The phone-call ended somewhat abruptly. "Yeah, ok, I'll talk to Dave and we'll be in touch." But that was the last I heard of it. I have never heard from Debbie since. The opportunity to host David Lee Roth's rock-climbing tour of Australia had been plonked right into my lap, and

I had dropped it stone cold. They were in another league. Ignorant of both Roth's fame and climbing interests, it all mattered little to me at the time. But when I told my brothers they laughed incredulously at my naivety. Who knows what might have come from it? There might have at least been money in it for me, perhaps even an opening into some kind of career in rock climbing adventure agency. Years later I learned that none other than Yosemite legend Ron Kauk had acted as chief rigger for Roth's photo shoot on Half Dome for his Skyscraper album, released in 1988, whose cover photo had been taken by Galen Rowell. The climbers had been rewarded with pay and a gold-plated karabiner to boot! It was only when I read Keith's Arapiles book, and saw Roth's grinning face in its pages, that I realized that he did make that visit to Arapiles after all. Who hosted and arranged it, I do not know. All I know is that Debbie's dead of night phone-call proved to be the moment in my life that I missed out on introducing a world superstar to Australia's greatest crag. Now that would have been something worth talking about!

Gearing up for a climb with Noddy at Arapiles.

CHAPTER FOUR

THE OUTDOOR ATHLETE

I think that the idea of seriously training for climbing first entered my mind thanks to Steve Ilg. His book, *The Outdoor Athlete*, arrived in my mailbox sometime in 1987 after many weeks of eager anticipation. Ilg was (and still is) a self-styled spiritual guru: on his current website he describes himself rather charmingly as "a very feeble mountain yogi/fitness monk." Although I found his idiosyncrasies endearing, had I read the more critical reviews that appeared soon after his book's publication, I might not have bought it. In the words of one reviewer, "Grotesque paragraphs, their meaning obscured by cascading rolls of verbal flab, lumber shamelessly through the book."[3]

Yet Ilg convinced me of a few important principles which have guided me ever since. First, he persuaded me to start squatting with a heavy barbell, a lesson that back in the day I suspect got me up big mountains in Peru and

---

[3] Richard Goldstone, in a review for the American Alpine Club.

which today, into my fifties, I continue to practise and value. Ilg also introduced me to a neat little circuit training routine that combined a suite of bodyweight strength moves performed at high intensity tempo. The circuit, at least in my modified and adapted form of it, consisted of a simple superset of five exercises: pullups, pushups, bench triceps, ab crunches, and split squat jumps. Each exercise was to be performed to what Ilg called MMF, momentary muscular failure. The set was followed by sixty seconds rest, then repeated for a total of three sets. I would often do this circuit having just run the seven kilometres home from work, already warm, loose, and a little taxed. As I improved I wore a pack for the pullups and pushups to add some resistance. Sometimes it burned and felt like I was dying (was it Ilg who told me to train through the burn, not to the burn?), but with the barbell squats it served as superb preparation for my 1989 expedition to Peru and in 1990 to the Diamond Couloir of Mt Kenya. Before that the only climbing-specific strength training I had done was weighted pullups and dips (I wanted triceps like Wolfgang Güllich's when he sent *Punks in the Gym* in 1985), so this represented a significant step forward. After Peru I got access to a gym and added a range of exercises to construct a regular strength training repertoire.

Ilg also stressed the need for mobility and good diet. For a while I adopted a virtually Pritikin diet of lentils and salad, though once I learned that Pritikin had died of a heart attack I lost some of my original enthusiasm. As for the lentils, besides giving me flatulence, a minor crisis at home put paid to them. I had put some on the stove to cook in one of my mother's good stainless steel pots and promptly forgot about them. Half an hour later clouds of smoke billowing from the kitchen into the lounge room alerted me to my unattended task. I spent several hours over many days scrubbing that pot, but it never found its original lustre. My mother, thankfully, was very forgiving.

As I hit middle-age I discovered the benefits of strength training combined with clean eating for fitness and mental health, joint and bone strength, and a healthy level of mass and power against the tide of natural muscular atrophy. Learning the olympic lifts in my mid-40s, the snatch and the clean and jerk, was an especial boon. These moves train the entire body and mind in synergy in the way they demand you to direct concentrated energy and power into a single, balanced, co-ordinated dynamic effort. They have direct carry over into almost any kind of athletic endeavour. Through the olympic lifts I have learned that strength is a skill: it can be trained and learned and practiced and applied with ever increasing success. And it is not just about strength. By scheduling higher volume training, using multiple sets of higher reps (without loss of form), an amazing level of cardio-vascular fitness can be reached just through these lifts and their supplementary exercises. As in my climbing grades, I never attained significant numbers in the olympic lifts, but I got serious enough to enter a number of state-level masters competitions. These events provided a goal to work towards, a test of my own progress and determination, just as an indoor climbing competition or mountain racing event might for the devoted climber. To this day my best lifts were made on the competition platform.

With strength training has come my share of overtraining and injury too. Hemorrhoids from heavy squatting; rotator cuff injury from behind the head pullups; a torn calf from uphill sprints; tendonitis in my elbows; chronic spondylolisthesis in my lumbar spine. Unwelcome as these have been, all can be accepted and viewed as pedagogical opportunities. Overtraining has taught me that when it comes to strength training, less is usually more, that the body has its own voice and wisdom to which the perceptive athlete will give due attention. Climbing has its own specific range of overtraining injuries, usually joint and tendon related. Long layoffs to give inflamed tendons or torn muscles time to recover can provoke depression and malaise. It's easy to lose motivation, or else, impatient with the enforced layoff, to get back into things too soon and relapse into further, possibly career-wrecking, injury. The climbing athlete, like the olympic weightlifter, needs to adopt a long-term approach to training: I am not training for tomorrow or even this weekend. I am training for next year, for the next decade, for middle and older age. You need to ask yourself:

do I still want to be climbing actively and well into my forties, fifties, and sixties? While it is important to be disciplined and not put off training when scheduled (and climbers are notoriously lazy, happy-go-lucky athletes), sometimes your body knows better. I don't mean you should skip training, but maybe you need to ease off the intensity or volume for that day, or schedule for an extra day per week of active recovery. As long as it follows hard and focused physical work, it is in fact while you are resting that true progress is made.

All the great masters of athletic formation know and teach these principles, having learned them mostly through trial and error, painful experience, and the university of hard knocks. Marc Twight, the once hard-core alpinist, has become an internationally acclaimed trainer, coach, and fitness mentor to hundreds of world class athletes using just these lessons, along with the relevant knowledge from the biophysical sciences. Another leading alpinist, Steve House, founder of *The Uphill Athlete* training resource company and now in his fifties, teaches similarly. Dan John and the late Dave Draper from the weightlifting world stand out as experts who know the wisdom of listening to the body and not being enslaved to equations, charts, prescriptions, cult fads and internet opinion. Chris Sharma, ranked among the top rock-climbers in the world, established his own gym brand devoted to climbing-specific training, all on the back of submitting to his own mentor and coach, who wisely steered him through a long and grueling regime to enable him to actualize undreamed-of possibilities.

To all these we could make additional reference to the growth of training literature that affirms the need for mental training and development. Climbing is very much a head game. Climbing coaches and authors like Arno Ilgner and Dave MacLeod have brought to heightened attention the obstacles to progress created by fear of falling and failure anxiety. In fact MacLeod claims that fear of falling is the primary weakness in over 50% of the climbers he coaches, and that confronting it requires not only practice in falling and targeted mental exercise, but "a dramatic reorientation towards what failure means."[4]

So now there is no excuse. In the 1980s we had Nathan Pritikin and Steve Ilg. Today every climber and outdoor athlete has a plethora of trainers and methods to choose from. The internet is saturated with information and guidance on training for climbing in all its various manifestations: gym, bouldering, crag, solo, waterfall, dry-tooling, alpine, high altitude and so on. Maybe that's the problem. Too much choice, too many options, cripple the mind and inhibit decision. With decision comes risk and responsibility, the very factors many

---

[4] Dave MacLeod, *9 out of 10 Climbers Make the Same Mistakes: Navigation through the Maze of Advice for the Self-Coached Climber* (Spean Bridge, Scotland: Rare Breed Productions, 2010), 12. See also Arno Ilgner, *The Rock Warrior's Way: Mental Training for Climbers* (La Vergen, Tennessee: Desiderata Institute, 2003).

young people fear the most. But when we accept risk and responsibility and move forward in action, we discover real freedom. There is no freedom in a plethora of choices, *per se*. There is only freedom in action. Should we settle for anything less?

One of the two olympic lifts, the snatch combines speed, strength, agility, and co-ordination in a single dynamic movement.

My brother Simon conjugating his Greek verbs on abseil at Onkaparinga, South Australia.

With Simon at Arapiles, 1987.

CHAPTER FIVE
ABSEIL FAIL AT THE ONKAS

We should have stayed home. It had been raining most of the night, and the showers hadn't really abated. But my brother Simon and I had been planning this little foray down to the crag in Onkaparinga Gorge for some time. We donned our rain jackets before hiking down from the car park, the misty damp cloud obscuring the view over the creek gorge below.

"Where's the track down?" called Simon. I didn't really know. But I had figured on abseiling down anyhow. "Why don't we rap down?" I replied. "Pretend we're in the mountains."

Simon didn't seem too confident. "You reckon? Looks pretty slippery."

I felt playful and adventurous. With the weather so crapped out, any decent climbing wasn't going to happen. I wanted instead to practise rope work, climbing wet slippery rock with a pack, maybe even use some pieces of aid, anything that might be useful training for alpine climbing. "Just imagine we're on the Eiger. Retreating in bad weather. I'll go down first with the pack. I can hold the rope while you rap down. That way you'll be safe."

I dumped the pack down on the muddy gravel and proceeded to pull out one of the two 8.5mm ropes and gear to set up an anchor around a fattish tree about five metres or so from the cliff's edge. The wind lashed light drizzly rain across our faces as we fiddled with our harnesses over our bulky jackets. I stuffed the rack and second rope and all the remaining kit back into the pack and slung it on my back. Like most trad cliff climbers, I was abseiling at this time with a simple figure 8 descender, without any form of third hand backup. To my mind, prussiks were for caving, glacier travel and crevasse rescue. I pushed the rope through and clipped in while the doubled fifty metre rope was still piled up on the ground next to me; then, having coiled the rope, called out "Rope!" and hurled it out and down into the cloudy void. Being so used to climbing at Morialta's short twelve to fifteen metre cliffs, I hadn't bothered tying a knot in the end, foolishly assuming the Onkaparinga climbs were of similar height. Just before leaning back, I asked Simon to check my set up. "Harness doubled back, screw gate tight, anchor looking good. You got everything you need? Ok, here I go, see you down the bottom."

It was an awkward lip, complicated by a thin wet rope and a heavy rucsac adding to my then already considerable hundred kilo frame. As I went over and into the vertical I soon found my feet and composure, but with the descender lacking friction in the wet I had to grip the doubled strands extra tight to keep control. I was about half-way down when the base of the cliff came into view. To my horror, I saw that the ends of the rope were dangling some fifteen to twenty feet from the ground. By the time I had grabbed the rope tightly enough to stop my descent, with some burn, I was only about six feet from abseiling off the ends into thin air, facing a fifteen-foot fall onto rocky, bone splitting ground.

Desperately I wrapped my right leg around the few spare feet of rope, locking myself enough to free a hand to tie a rough overhand knot with the loose ends of the rope. But even a biggish knot will pull through a figure eight descender, especially with 8.5mm rope. I lashed the rope more tightly around my leg, trying to halt the inch-by-inch slip through the descender. Meanwhile the weight of the pack was pulling me backwards, forcing me to use one hand on the upper part of the rope to keep myself upright, while my feet, still in runners, slipped around on the wet muddy rock, searching unsuccessfully for purchase to ease my weight. During my descent, the rain had picked up, and a stream of water started flowing down the rope, soaking my hands and harness.

"Hey Adam! You there yet?" Simon's voice echoed down the cliff. "Umm! I'm stuck!" I cried out. "The rope doesn't reach the ground. I'm stuck. I'm gonna need you to help me. Right now. Quickly! You need to lower a rope down to me!" No sooner had I said those words when I realized the spare rope was in the pack on my back.

You can probably imagine the scene: how I wrestled the pack off my back and managed somehow to clip it to my harness; how I extracted the rope and a prussik; how I dropped the rope to the ground; how Simon slipped and scrambled down the wet descent track to the base of the route to fetch the rope, then back up again to secure it to the tree. How in the meantime I tied a prussik to secure myself to the rope and waited for Simon to rig up a belay and send down the rope with ready-made bight and carabiner to clip in to; how he lowered me to the bottom, relieved but soaked, muddied, and above all, chastened by my misjudgement.

If I remember rightly, Simon actually ended up leading a nice little route that day, in the wet, holds slimed with dirty grit. I don't think I followed, opting instead to scramble up the track to the side. I wasn't too shaken, but I had learned a lesson. Unless you can see both ends of the rope on the ground, with slack to spare, always tie a knot in the end of your abseil rope. Unfortunately it took a somewhat uncontrolled speedy and slippy sticht-plate rap down a thin rope on the Cosmiques Arete on the Aiguille de Midi many years later to learn the further lesson that, for both crags and mountains, you should always use a "third hand" prussik backup.

All that happened in 1993. It could have been much worse. I don't think I would have died. But it would surely have ended in broken bones. I've only been back to the Onkas once since, on a hot summer's day, with both Simon and our oldest brother Michael, and with leisure enough to swim afterwards in the long dark pool in the creek below, under the sweet cooling shadows of the gum trees.

Malcolm Matheson (HB) onsighting *Hindley Shuffle* (27), Norton Summit, 1989.

HB surveying the damage after the climb.

CHAPTER SIX
CHANNEL NINE AT MORIALTA

During our years of undergraduate study and vocational training in the early 1990s, my brothers Simon and James and I appeared three times on Channel Nine's *Hey, Hey It's Saturday* for the *Red Faces* variety show. *Hey Hey* was immensely popular in its day. It ran for some twenty-nine years, during which it clocked up over 500 episodes and won nineteen Logie Awards. At its peak it attracted over two and a half million viewers, surpassing ratings of top current shows like *Masterchef*, *The Block*, *Married at First Sight* and *My Kitchen Rules*. The *Red Faces* segment on *Hey Hey* attracted little real talent. Being a spoof of real talent shows, it wasn't meant to. But there were some exceptions, including leading actress Cate Blanchett, who appeared on the show when she was just 17. My brothers too were (and still are) both gifted musicians, so while we were there purely for the fun, we actually won first place two out of the three times, receiving a high score once from guest judge Russell Crowe and twice from the normally severe regular judge Red Symons. The welcome prize money paid for much-needed books and tuition, and the TV appearances won us a certain dubious celebrity among our disbelieving peers.

A few years after our *Red Faces* appearances, Channel Nine in Melbourne got in touch with us about sending a crew over to Adelaide to interview and film us for their *Red Faces* spin-off show *Gonged But Not Forgotten*, a kind of bio-documentary series based on old *Red Faces* acts and hosted by comedian Peter Rowsthorn. Besides filming us at our respective places of work, Peter and his crew requested a full day to shoot a group interview. Given our shared fraternal interest in climbing we selected the cliffs at Morialta Falls as our preferred location, with a rock climb to serve as the main visual feature.

The day dawned sunny and clear. We met the crew at the top of the cliffs on the Norton Summit road and toted all the gear, which included Simon's guitar, down the track towards the crags. It was slow and awkward getting the camera and sound man down the descent track with all their equipment, but eventually we had all our people and kit safely down at the base of the orange wall at Boulder Bridge. While they set up we began laying out all the gear from our climbing packs and putting on our harnesses. Peter came over and started inspecting our stuff, fascinated by the rack. "What do you call these things?" he asked, fingering a carabiner.

"That's a carabiner, or crab."

"A crab? Okay. Doesn't look like a crab. And what about these?" He pointed to a Wild Country friend.

"Ahh, that's called a friend", came the reply.

"A friend? Are you serious? Why do you need so many? I guess doing this sort of thing you could use a few", he joked. "What are they for?"

"Well, you squeeze this trigger-thing here, like a syringe, and the front cams narrow, like this. Then you push it into a crack in the rock and let go, and it jams tight, like this." I placed the camming device into a nearby slot. "Then you clip a quickdraw or the rope into the crab and you can use it to make an anchor or protect yourself on the climb."

Peter looked on amazed, my jargon lost on him but the demonstration apparently making some sense. Chalk bags, harnesses, nuts, wires, hexes, crabs, friends, quickdraws, belay devices, nut removing tool, helmets, ropes, shoes, slings, bolt plates: all the familiar business of a complete trad rack were splayed over the flat rock before him. "Wow! I guess all this lot cost a fair bit?" he asked as he moved back, stepping onto the rope draped over a rock. "Ahh, yes. I'll just move that rope.... Yeah, it's not cheap stuff. But your life can depend on it, so you want to make sure it's up to scratch."

The first few shots were of Peter introducing the surrounds and the plan for the climb. He donned a helmet for the sequence, his already big ears accentuated by the smooth bowl of the lid. We decided that Simon would lead *Muesli*, a classic eighteen metre grade 16 arete first put up by Colin Reece and Mike Round in 1972. The crew would film the lead from the ground. Then they would shift the camera to the top of the cliff to get a few shots of me following, before a final set of shots of the three of us sitting under the sheoak at the top of the orange wall singing a song accompanied by Simon on his guitar.

For us the climbing was enjoyable but pretty uneventful. There were the usual safety and belay calls, along with the odd shout of encouragement. Occasionally Simon called out for slack, commented on possible protection or made some exclamation when dealing with a difficult or exposed move. Peter, picking up on our verbal exchanges, poked fun at how calmly we were facing the challenges of the vertical terrain. With his helmet pulled hard down on his ears, he leaned close into the camera and whispered in a hoarse voice. "The great thing about watching a couple of Lutheran priests rock-climb is that when things get a bit stressful, instead of blaspheming or swearing, they go, 'Golly gosh', 'Oooh', 'Hooley dooley!' All the big ones, yeah, they use 'em, they're not scared!"

With the climbing over, the final request was for the three of us to sit on the edge of the cliff with our legs hanging over the orange wall. The interview, filmed just back from the edge, focused on our childhood days in Papua New Guinea and East Africa, our love for climbing and adventure and making music, and the apparent contradiction between our *Red Faces* acts and our more serious roles in pastoral care and hospital chaplaincy. After they shifted the camera position back to take in the drop, we sat down and strummed our song. With the midday sun beaming brightly over the beige-orange rock and the valley below, we sang Paul McCartney's *Mull of Kintyre* to Simon's guitar, breaking into a crisp three-part harmony for the chorus and looking out over the bush covered hills.

> *Far have I travelled and much have I seen*
> *Darkest of mountains and valleys of green.*
> *Past painted deserts the sun sets on fire*
> *As he carries me home to the Mull of Kintyre.*

Peter and the crew were thrilled. They had got what they came for. It had been a colourful two days and all had gone like clockwork. These days climbing is all over the news and media. Everyone is doing it, thanks to the explosion of indoor walls, school climbing programs, professional instruction and commercial groups. But twenty-five years ago it was regarded as a bizarre and exotic novelty, the pursuit of freaks and death-wishers. It was probably not the first time a camera crew had filmed climbers at Morialta, but as far as the Channel Nine team knew it was a first for a national-level prime time entertainment show. Their job now was to head back to Melbourne and edit the two days of filming into a 30 minute segment in time to take it to air in the next month or two.

Looking back now I realize that it was a significant historical moment. Without trying to orchestrate anything, still less deserving of any fame, my brothers and I had played a small part in propelling climbing along the path towards its present-day popularity. Whether that was a good or bad thing, I'm not sure. Certainly there were others in the Adelaide climbing scene far more qualified and able to do so. Nonetheless, we were still laughing with incredulity as we wound our way down the Norton Summit road, car windows down, with the afternoon sun in our faces, the warm northwest wind tussling our hair, the picture of the crag fresh in our minds and the lyrics of our song reverberating in our ears:

> *Smiles in the sunshine and tears in the rain*
> *Still take me back where my memories remain*
> *Flickering embers go higher and higher*
> *As they carry me back to the Mull of Kintyre.*

CHAPTER SEVEN

AVALANCHED ON MT COOK

In the spring season of 1987 I spent two months ski-touring and climbing in the Mt Cook region of New Zealand. I arrived at the Mt Cook Youth Hostel without a partner, and over the following weeks teamed up with a varying range of climbers, misfits, and wanna-bes like me. Among the climbers I remember Heinz Schwarz, the Swiss mountain guide who had climbed the Eiger Nordwand. Together we went up the Beetham Valley and climbed Aiguille Rouge. Another was Paul Horne, an Australian entomologist who had wintered in Antarctica, and with whom I spent a week climbing various routes from Mueller Hut. Paul and I went on to forge a brief but solid partnership, culminating in our Diamond Couloir expedition on Mt Kenya in 1990. Yet another was Uli, at that time co-manager of the new YHA hostel in Mt Cook.

Early one morning we raced off on a fitness run to the Copeland Pass. It was Uli's first time in crampons, and coming down from the pass he slipped, somehow managing in the panic to arrest his slide with his ice-axe. We took a wrong turn in cloud past the shelter on the way down and got waylaid, but needless to say we were back in the Mt Cook pub by opening time to celebrate our success.

Another unforgettable outing took place with legendary Twizel mountain guide Shaun Norman and an American client of his by the name of Tom. Tom had engaged Shaun to guide him up Mt Cook via the Linda Glacier route on touring skis. In the days prior to their trip, Tom and I had teamed up to do some cragging and fitness hikes in the surrounding hills. We negotiated for me to accompany them on their flight into Plateau Hut, spend a day assisting them practice some crevasse rescue, leave them to their climb while I fiddled around skiing around Glacier Dome and Mt Dixon, then ski out with them via Cinerama Col and down Boys Glacier and the Tasman to the road-end past Ball Hut.

It turned out that Tom was not as fit as he needed to be to ski up the Linda. Maybe he was freaked out by the scale of the looming seracs. The day spent doing crevasse rescue had exhausted him. Looking out from our vantage point near the base of Mt Dixon across the vista presented by the avalanche-raked faces of Mt Tasman and Mt Silberhorn, the serac-threatened Linda Glacier, the long

Zurbriggen Ridge, the enormous east face and east ridge of Mt Cook down to the vast cirque of Grand Plateau spilling into the Hochstetter icefall, Tom looked puffy and overwhelmed. Even so, he had paid a lot of money to be there, so that night at two a.m. he and Shaun set off in perfect conditions.

By lunch-time from the summit of Glacier Dome, sitting in the snow with my bare skin soaking up the gammas, I saw their two tiny figures skinning slowly back across the plateau. They had got fairly high on the Linda, zig zagging their way up through the deep spring snow on skins, but were too late to attempt the rock band below the summit ice cap. Having met them back at Plateau Hut, we made ready for an immediate ski-out, with Shaun aiming to reach the radio at Ball Hut in time to call Alpine Guides before they shut shop at five p.m. to arrange a ride and spare us the long fifteen-kilometre walk-out.

By the time we reached Cinerama Col, with the daunting 7000 foot Caroline Face of Mt Cook alongside us, it was obvious we were going to have to hurry to reach Ball Hut by five p.m.. With our skins peeled and stowed, Shaun asked me to bring up the rear and pressed on ahead around the base of Anzac Peaks and down the slopes of Boys Glacier, soon disappearing beyond view. Tom struggled to ski under the weight of his pack, falling often in the deep snow, then flailing around like an upturned turtle trying to get on his feet again. As the slope steepened, Tom was forced to ski in long diagonal traverses across the slope, while I waited for him to get down enough to resume my own descent.

It was there on the southern edge of Boys Glacier that the avalanche happened. Tom was on his back again, pack beneath him, wrestling to right himself with his poles. A long crack appeared in the snow above and around him as the slab he was sitting on gave way. He slid down the slope on a massive carpet of moving snow, looking around helplessly with surprised shock.

"Stop! Stop! Save yourself!" I screamed out, realizing the futility of my words even as I said them. Tom by now had rolled onto his front, and was clawing desperately at the collapsing snow pack, trying to halt his slide. The avalanche had picked up speed, and the snow was crumbling into heavy fluidity, narrowing like a river as it funneled towards the rocky outcrop below. Tom's body had sunk into the advancing waves of snow, half buried in their depths. His arms had stopped moving and he appeared resigned to certain death. But as the avalanche funneled into the rock gully, its pace slowed and the snow jammed up on itself, momentarily blocking its cascading descent. I began to ski down towards Tom, who had come to a stop just metres above the drop. Getting his pack off, I helped him to his feet. Recovering a buried ski and pole, we half skied, half scrambled off to the left onto firmer snow, out of harm's way. From here I spied Shaun about two hundred metres below, looking up and waiting to see what the hold-up was. He had seen the avalanche running over the rock outcrop and was wondering what the hell had happened.

It took a while to regroup and recover. Shaun skied quickly back up to us while I sat Tom down and plied him with drink and food. Meanwhile I started transferring part of his load into my pack: sleeping bag and mat, helmet, crampons and axes. On his arrival Shaun loaded up the other half, until Tom's pack was nearly empty. It was about four p.m. This time Shaun stayed with Tom, while I headed off down the slopes, ungainly under the additional load, angling across toward the base of Ball Glacier.

I made the radio call by five p.m. Someone promised to send a car and driver. It was well after dark by the time we got to the road end. Tom slumped down into the back seat while we loaded up the skis and packs. As the car rumbled down the rough road, I imagined his troubled thoughts. He had nearly died in an avalanche. I remembered how helpless I had felt, watching him slide away, and thought how ridiculous had been my cries for him to save himself from such a mighty, mindless force. Once again I had returned from the mountains enchanted by their power and splendor, humiliated by my vulnerability, relieved and thankful to be alive.

Shaun Norman and Tom on the summit of Glacier Dome near Plateau Hut, New Zealand, 1987.

The view across the Grand Plateau from Cinerama Col, New Zealand. Tom took this photo on my camera not long before the avalanche.

CHAPTER EIGHT

THIN ICE IN THE ROCKIES

Quebecois climber Serge Angelucci has been at the forefront of extreme waterfall climbing and alpinism for three decades in the Rockies, Baffin Island, Greenland, the Alps and the Himalayas. Even today, in his late fifties, Serge's name appears in climbing annals with new and difficult routes besides his name. Back in 1990 he appeared in the climbing movie *A bout de glace* with French alpinist Francois Damilano, with whom he has pioneered numerous hard routes in Canada and Europe. A few years later Serge teamed up with Jeff Everett to send a variant on *The Terminator* which at that time was possibly the most visionary and difficult big ice climb in the Canadian Rockies. The ascent was filmed and circulated in the movie *Walking on Ice*. There's a great photo of Serge hanging off *Icetroman* (M8 R) on the front cover of the French-Canadian climbing magazine *Le*

Mousqueton 28/4 (1998). When he first sent it in 1996 it was the first M8 ice-route in Quebec.

I had the privilege of climbing with Serge when I was in Banff for the winter of 1987-1988. I met him by accident, I think, when he was in Banff doing some illegal carpentry work for cash at a building site, and I was hanging around looking for a climbing partner. My friend Jim Baker had let me sleep on the floor in his condominium and given me liberal use of his car to go climbing or skiing, but Jim himself was busy managing Monod's ski store twelve hours a day, seven days a week. Serge had an old tank of a car, and though it was less reliable than Jim's more luxurious cruiser, we only resorted to Jim's car when temperatures dropped below minus fifteen and Serge's wouldn't start.

Serge and I were both living on a shoestring budget. During December I lived rent-free at Jim's place, but his landlord started asking questions so in January I moved to the Hostel up on Tunnel Mountain. I was able to get an evening job there in the kitchen washing dishes, which paid for my bed and gave me daytimes and weekends to climb. By living on peanut butter and jam sandwiches and vegetables salvaged from the bins at the back of Safeway I was able to splurge on a new Stubai ice hammer to replace my retarded Camp alpine hammer. The Stubai had a multi-function head with spare pick. It paired nicely with my Chouinard axe. Serge's carpentry job dried up for the Christmas vacation, so he only had enough money for petrol. For a couple of weeks his climbing kit was cobbled together from who knows where. For boots he used an old pair of ski boots, which set his lower legs at such a forward angle that he was often banging his knees on steep ice and losing purchase on his front points. His ice tools had huge coarse teeth that made extraction laborious. On harder pitches when he was leading I would offer him my Stubai hammer which, with its heavy head, placed very cleanly and with its finely serrated teeth extracted effortlessly. For protection I had three Chouinard ice screws, two bang-in snargs, a warthog, and a soft Russian 'titanium' screw.

Our first climb together was Professor Falls. It was there that I learned that Serge didn't care much for formal climbing calls and belay communication. When he got to the top of a pitch, I learned to wait for him just to pull hard on the rope. That was my signal to climb. At first I had tried nervously to ensure that I was on belay. "Serge, am I on belay?!" I would shout out. "Ok! Climbing! Am I on belay?" But after several attempts with no reply, I would just entrust myself to a moving rope and climb on up.

Once, on Cascade Falls, I had just led a pitch and was setting up the anchor for a belay. I had already clipped into a good screw and called "Safe", and so expected Serge to be cleaning the belay below and getting himself ready for my shout of, "On belay, climb when ready!" With the anchor ready I started pulling in slack rope, waiting for it to tighten up so I could clip it to my belay device. Instead, after pulling in a few lengths of slack rope, I heard picks on ice, then saw Serge's head appear at the edge of the belay ledge. He had climbed the entire pitch without any belay. He must have started climbing while I had still been finishing my own lead. Stunned with dismay, I didn't know whether to apologize for failing to belay him or berate him for climbing in synch without letting me know. Either way he had put the anchors at risk in case of a long fall. But Serge just smiled and proceeded to climb through unapologetically, not even bothering to take the extra screws off my harness. He just assumed I'd sort out the belay as he climbed. It was only Grade 3 ice and I guess he was confident that I, like him, wouldn't fall off.

Another memorable day with Serge was on Bourgeau Lefthand, a 600-foot Grade 5 ice smear on steep rock below a massive avalanche bowl near Sunshine Ski Field. The ice during the winter of 1987-88 was not particularly thick, and when we got to the base of the climb we saw that that our route consisted of a two-metre wide, one inch plaster of ice with a hollow backside. The entire slab looked like it might fall off with the slightest weight, and as Serge started up the first pitch, his ice tools made dreadful hollow echoing sounds as he gingerly hooked them in and transferred his weight to them. The only screw he placed about thirty feet up went in about four inches before it hit rock, with just the first inch of the screw in contact with ice. I was relieved when at about fifty feet Serge declared in his heavy Quebecois accent,

"Thee hice here, he is very thin." With some coaxing, I persuaded him to come down, and we headed off to Johnston Canyon for a consolation climb. I'm pretty sure I didn't do anything to advance Serge's world-class climbing career, but I sometimes tell myself that I maybe kept him alive long enough to have one.

Serge Angelucci approaching Borgeau Falls, Canadian Rockies, 1987.

Serge on the cover of *Le Mousqueton*, the Montreal-based climbing magazine.

CHAPTER NINE

THE WOLF

There is another story to tell about a day out with Serge. One morning we were driving along the Banff-Jasper Highway on our way to climb Weeping Wall near the Columbia Icefields. Weeping Wall is one of the best known and most road-accessible ice-climbs in Canada. In the winter of 1987-1988 it was comparatively thin, with only one or two climbable lines in the lower 550 foot-high tier. I had made a first attempt in early December, but beyond the first pitch it proved unclimbable. It was now January, and we had heard that the lower tier was better formed and inviting ascents.

There was a thin layer of fresh un-ploughed snow over the road and traffic was scarce. As the highway opened before us, flanked either side by forest and spectacular mountains, we noticed far ahead something on the road. Serge slowed down and we coasted the last few yards to pull up in front of a plump freshly-killed bird. With the car stopped and engine running, we hopped out and inspected the body, finding it still soft and warm. Serge picked it up and held it in his hands. "Ha! A groose!", he declared.

"A grouse? Really? Wow! It must have just been hit by a car," I said. "It's still warm." It was actually a ptarmigan, but it fit the bill of an edible game bird.

"I will take him", said Serge. "My girlfriend, she will cook him. Groose his very nice." He opened the trunk of his car and laid the bird carefully on a plastic shopping bag, smudging it with blood.

Just as Serge closed the boot and we stepped back towards the open doors, we both noticed that we were being watched. To the right of the road, just at the edge of the trees where the verge meets the forest, there stood a lone timber wolf. It had been watching us the whole time, stock still, as we had taken its meal off the road and stowed it in the back of our car. It was a majestic sight. It stood motionless, fearless, condensed breath issuing silently from its nostrils. With a large hungry wolf only twenty yards away, I should have felt apprehensive. Instead I was awestruck with wonder, momentarily enchanted by this mysterious, lonely creature with its intelligent, penetrating gaze. After what seemed like minutes, with Serge and me saying nothing, the wolf turned and trotted soundlessly away into the forest, disappearing into its snowy depths. When it had gone, after a moment of silent watching, we turned and looked at each other, knowing without words that we had witnessed something special, yet feeling guilty that we had interrupted its intentions and stolen away its prey.

A couple of hours later we were engrossed in the challenge of working our way up the Grade 5 four-pitch tier of Weeping Wall. The climb was satisfying in every respect: shared leads; solid belays; long vertical sections; variable ice – sometimes thick and plastic, sometimes thin, delicate and hollow; the cave crux through untouched chandelier ice; the abseil descent down Sniveling Gully to the left. But through it all, and ever since, the splendid and haunting vision of that solitary wolf, master of the forest, never left me.

Climbing partner Bill following on Grotto Falls, Canadian Rockies, 1988.

Serge climbing Borgeau Falls, Canadian Rockies.

CHAPTER TEN

MT ANDROMEDA FAIL

One of my last forays into the mountains during my 1987-1988 winter in Banff was a half-baked attempt on the classic Skyladder route on Mt Andromeda (11,318 ft) in the Columbia Icefields. The plan had been for Jim and me to make the two and a half hour drive up from Banff after Jim had knocked off work at Monod's, bivvy in the carpark at the mouth of the Athabasca Glacier, then set off around three a.m. for what we expected to be a solid eight to twelve hour round trip. To add to the fun, Serge and a mate of his were going to come along as well, in their own car, to try the much more difficult Andromeda Strain, a formidable winter test-piece. The idea was for all four of us to meet in the carpark, walk in together, split up for our respective climbs, then gather on the summit and return to celebrate.

It was midnight by the time Jim and I parked in the carpark at the end of the road. There in the bleak darkness stood Serge's car, but there was no one to be seen, and the wind had swept away any footprints in the snow. Jim and

I wriggled into our sleeping bags, hoping to get some shut-eye between then and our scheduled wake-up time. But in the cramped car, and with the frigid wind buffeting the iced-up windows, sleep was impossible. Restless, I switched on my headlight and clawed around in my food bag, pulling out a stick of salami and a tin of sardines. Both were frozen. Thankfully I had put an apple inside my sleeping bag with my water bottle, preserving both from solidification.

It was a relief to step out into the wind at three a.m. and stretch out into our approach walk along the top of the moraine wall on the left side of the glacier. The snow sparkled and glistened under the beam of our headlamps, and our boots sunk deeply into the snowdrift, the arctic gusts blasting away the loose spindrift released by our steps. Not far along, a hulking orange shape came into view: it was a huge, abandoned snowcat bus, its tracks buried in drift. Once these had been used to cart tourists up the glacier, but had been replaced by the new Brewster coaches with the giant tyres. It sat looking cold and forlorn in the dark night, silent witness to a bygone era.

Soon the approach started meandering under the north facing slopes of the Athabasca massif to our left. The wind had deposited tonnes of snow over these angled slopes, and we began to feel uneasy about the stability of the pack. We found ourselves sinking ever more deeply with each step, breaking through the wind-crusted surface. We were only a few yards apart when all of a sudden we heard and felt a shuddering "whumph!" in the snow pack beneath us. My immediate reaction was to turn and run, down and away from any advancing avalanche. Jim stood his ground, and after a few moments I stopped and turned to survey the slope. "What the hell was that?" I shouted out through the wind. "I don't know but it didn't sound good!" called Jim, as he plodded back down to join me.

For the next five minutes or so we consulted, casting our headlight beams around on the snowy slopes above us and trying to assess the relative risk of avalanche. In my understanding, lee slopes were susceptible to wind-slab build-up. The "whumph" we had heard was the classic sound of a slab of snow shifting under weight, often the trigger precipitating its break and slide from the harder pack beneath. It was hard to work out where the leeside was in our current situation. High above, the north facing Silberhorn Face of Athabasca was bare of snow altogether, scoured by winds down to hard ice. But here, with the wind funneling down the glacier and swirling in and around the moraine wall, there were leeside drifts in multiple directions, none of them of massive acreage, but all worrying enough for a night-time approach in unfamiliar terrain along a route neither of us had been on.

Eventually we decided to head back to the car, about an hour away. In face of the icy wind and possible avalanche risk, without touring skis, and with no sign of Serge and his mate other than an empty car, our motivation had dwindled. Back in the car out of the wind, we figured we might as well sit tight until light, just in case the others showed up. But at dawn there was still no sign, so before heading off down the Icefields Parkway, we stuck a folded note under their windscreen wiper, telling them we would meet them back in Banff that evening.

I can't remember how we spent that day. Did we go skiing or climbing somewhere? Or did we just head home and snooze? I don't recall. I do remember, however, how we caught up with Serge and his friend later that evening. They had had little more success than we. In an odd coincidence, it turned out that they had been sleeping in the old abandoned snowcat when we had gone past both ways, oblivious. They had waited there until light before starting out on their own climb, but had turned back when they got freaked out by the crevasses on the slopes below their route.

A few years passed before Serge eventually got his success on Andromeda Strain. In 1994 he headed back to the Columbia Icefields with French guides Christophe Moulin and Richard Ouairy. According to Chic Scott's account in his book *Pushing the Limits*, the trio "left Canmore in the early hours, raced at 160 kph up the Icefields Parkway, climbed *The Andromeda Strain*, and were back in Canmore for happy hour!"[5]

---

[5] Chic Scott, *Pushing the Limits: The Story of Canadian Mountaineering* (Calgary, Alberta: Rocky Mountain Books, 2000), 409.

CHAPTER ELEVEN

DEATH ON ALPAMAYO

My first attempt on Alpamayo (5947m) in the Peruvian Andes was a failure. Irishman Tony Duboudin and I arrived at basecamp with an arriero (donkey driver) and two burros loaded with kit and food after an epic trek. Starting up the Quebrada Llanganuco, we had made a successful side-trip climb to the summit of Nevado Pisco (5752m), then hiked over the Portachuelo de Llanganuco down to Colcabamba village, on to the spectacular Punta Union pass, and finally down the Santa Cruz valley. We were fit and acclimatized and expectations were high. For me it was the culminating point of eighteen months' preparation going back to a conversation with Kiwi Anton Wopereis in Banff in 1987. Anton had held a slide night at Jim Baker's place displaying exploits from recent trips to Peru and the French Alps. His photos of steep alpine ice on Les Droites' north face and Alpamayo's southwest face were inspirational. Having climbed together at Lake Louise and Grotto Falls, Anton assured me that I was more than capable for Alpamayo.

International trekking guide Val Pitkethli had also been at the slideshow, and she had promised to provide contacts and support for any Peru trip I might plan.

Val's organizational skills ended up proving invaluable.[6] I arrived jet-lagged in Lima in May 1989 to taxi straight to the Hotel San Francisco which Val had recommended. My first acclimatization ascent up Huamashraju (5434m) just east of Huaraz was achieved with her and local climber Jorque just four days after my arrival in Huaraz. She introduced me to all the best and safest places to eat in town. Once I teamed up with Tony, Val continued to help with arriero contacts and logistical support.

Our charged emotions on our arrival at the green meadow of Alpamayo's basecamp were soon dampened by news of a fatality on the French direct on the southwest face, the very route we were attempting. While we unloaded our burros and began setting up tents, a group of rescuers were loading up a horse with the wrapped corpse of the dead climber. As the horse was led past our camp we saw the stockinged feet of the victim dangling loose outside the blanket. His body hung stiffly over the horse's back, bouncing awkwardly with its gait. It was a sobering moment.

---

[6] She has since written and published a guidebook based on her long experience in the region. See Val Pitkethly and Kate Harper, *Trekking and Climbing in the Andes* (2002).

It wasn't until later, blizzarded in our snowcave at the high camp near the face at 5400 metres, that we learned from two similarly ensconced Canadians the details of the accident. Three Swiss climbers had been high on the French route, with the leader on the last pitch just about to tackle the huge summit cornice. Suddenly the cornice collapsed and swept down the entire route, scouring it clear of snow down to bare black and blue ice. The lead climber was killed, his body buried under debris near the base of the route. A second climber was also swept down the route, pulling his anchor and ending up in a crevasse some one hundred metres below the bergschrund. Amazingly, he suffered only concussion and a broken leg. The third climber was left stranded at 19,000 feet with a shredded rope and some 1500 feet of 70-80 degree angled hard ice below him. He managed to downclimb to safety.

The Canadians had witnessed the calamity and stitched together a rescue to get the surviving climbers down. The body was retrieved just before a week of bad weather rolled in, making our attempt untenable. For three nights we sat in our snow cave, dug laboriously with a pot lid after a regrettable decision not to bring the tent in order to save weight. In the white-out conditions we made a half-hearted attempt on Quitaraju (6040m), but got lost on the glacier on the approach. With our food and fuel all used up, we retreated back down to the Santa Cruz valley and out to Huaraz, disappointed, but happy to be alive.

About a week later, just before returning to Alpamayo for what became a successful attempt on the Italian route, we saw a hotel notice-board advertising a pile of assorted climbing gear for sale. It included a couple of bent ice screws, one crampon, a tent, alpine clothing, freeze-dried food, and several picks and axes. It was the gear salvaged by locals from the Swiss climbers' tragedy. I thought of the dead man's parents, their grief at hearing the news and trying to get his body home. I thought of my own parents back in Adelaide, and prayed not to die, if only to spare them the same unspeakable loss.

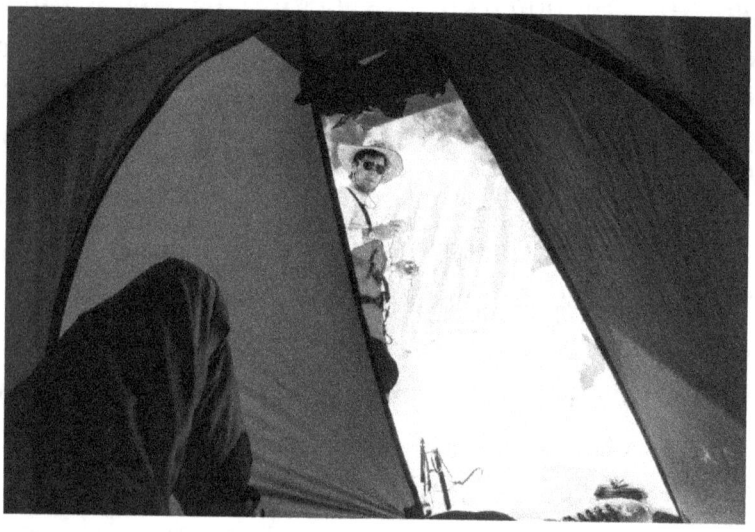

Tony and the fluted south-west face of Alpamayo (5947m), framed by our tent door. This was on our second, successful attempt.

CHAPTER TWELVE
THE MOUNTAIN LION

I saw the mountain lion at the head of the Quebrada Ishinca in Peru. Or rather it saw me. Tony and I had just failed on Toclaraju (6032m) and were bashing down the track through the moraine. We had left our arriero and burros in the Ishinca valley two days before, headed for the high camp on the saddle at 5300 metres with sights on either the west face or the northwest ridge, but made a wrong turn above the moraine. The mistake had cost us a full day. We had traversed west in deep snow around the wrong side of the spurs on the Toclaraju-Urus ridge to find ourselves on a totally different part of the mountain, somewhere on the northeast side of Urus Este, and at least a good four hours away from where we had intended to end up. We were forced to camp on a shoulder of snow and, having enjoyed a glorious sunset with spectacular views over Laguna Aquilpo, dourly endured a wasted night.

The next day had been spent in regaining our original route. Although the way was technically straightforward, it had almost ended in disaster. Moving un-roped up a hard snow slope of about 45 degrees, I had arrived at a rock band, beneath which we needed to traverse eastwards to reach our ridge. Steadying myself with my free hand on the broken rock to kick a step in the snow, the huge boulder on which my hand was resting suddenly dislodged and fell solidly across my legs, knocking me off my stance and sending me into an awkward slide. Amazingly, my cramponed boots caught sharply in the frozen surface and lurched me upright, while the boulder, about the size of small fridge, bounced and skittered off at a frightening rate straight towards Tony, who was some hundred metres away down the slope. I screamed "Rock!" just in time for him to look up and take guard. The boulder whizzed by him, about ten feet shy, and blasted its way down the snow slope until it disappeared with loud explosive cracks among the rocks at the base.

As Tony cramponed up to me, I inspected my legs. My gaiter and goretex pants had been ripped open, and my calf was grazed and bleeding slightly, but there was no real cut. Oddly, my gloves were also ripped and my finger and knuckles were bleeding and bruised, though I don't remember how this happened. Had I not immediately righted myself as I had, it would have been difficult self-arresting on such a hard surface.

From here we reached our intended camp on the broad exposed snowfield without incident, set on the glacial saddle beneath the west face and north-west ridge. We pitched our tent alongside an amazing bottomless crevasse in which we spent the afternoon ice-bouldering. Its smooth, dead vertical sides, which went back as far as the eye could see, stood parallel about six feet apart, and there was a way to walk in and out from the side via a snow ramp. The entire crevasse was quite dark, being roofed above with an arched snow bridge, but reflected light entered through the ramp opening off the side. Looking into its vast depths gave us the willies: our headlights searched in vain for the bottom, and despite the secure placement of our tools in the deep glacial ice, we mostly used a belay rope, going in one at a time while the other belayed off a bombproof screw at the edge of the ramp.

When we finally emerged from the crevasse around five p.m. it was snowing. Ensconced in our sleeping bags in the tent, we melted snow and cooked up some soup and noodles, followed by numerous cups of tea while we played rounds of cribbage. Feeling sleepy, Tony pulled the hood of his sleeping bag up around his ears and began to hum and sing to himself in a soft, quasi-toneless voice. One song was an old Irish lullaby he learned from his mother:

> *When midnight comes, and people homeward tread,*
> *Seek out their blankets and their feather bed,*
> *Home comes the rover, his journey's over.*
> *Yield up the night-time to old John-o-dream.*

Eventually around nine he rolled over and fell immediately into heavy sleep, while I pulled out a tattered novel, *Night Without End*, by Alistair Maclean. The snow continued to fall heavily, its patter audible on the taught tent nylon. The aptly-titled novel gripped me, and I read by headlight long into the night. Once during the night, while out to relieve myself, I had to sweep a foot of snow off the tent roof with my gloved hands and clear away the mouth of the vestibule. It seemed clear that the climb was off. I finished my novel around three a.m., my headlight battery almost dead, and with sore eyes and vivid snowy images from the novel whirling around my mind, drifted into a fitful sleep.

In the morning, crisp cold air and a clear, windless sky filled us momentarily with re-awakened hope. It quickly evaporated when a massive rumble from nearby overwhelmed the loud chugging of my MSR stove. We looked out through the open tent vestibule to see a huge avalanche thundering down the west face of Toclaraju, sweeping across the approach route to the northwest ridge. "Oi tink dat just about tells us everythin' we need to know about da snow conditions on da route," Tony observed wryly, as he turned his attention back to the pot of snow melting on the roaring stove.

So it was that we packed up and headed back down to the Quebrada Ishinca. I broke trail through deep snow, ploughing down the glacier without pause towards the start of the track at the top of the rocky moraine. When I reached it, I looked back to check on Tony. I had been preoccupied during the descent and hadn't noticed that he had fallen way behind; indeed, he appeared to have stopped. I took off my pack and sat down on a rock at the moraine edge, sipping from my water bottle, chewing on some rat-gnawed brazil nuts, and taking in the view southwards towards the rising bulk of Ranrapalca. Further below and west in the meadows of the upper Ishinca valley lay our base camp attended by our burro driver. I enjoyed the welcome spell. After about ten minutes, I looked back up towards Tony only to discover that he hadn't budged. He appeared to be sitting back in the snow looking at the clouds.

It took a lot of frustrated shouting back and forth and wild hand waving to confirm that he was alright. Apparently he was just taking his time and enjoying the scene. I was a bit miffed as I loaded up and headed off down the zig-zag track through the moraine, wondering where this Irishman had got his mountain sense from. My frustration was partly motherly concern. What if he took a slide and smashed his head up on the moraine? Who would know? Who would help him? I wondered aloud whether he had any thought for moving quickly, sticking together, or, even more basically, communicating to his partner what in heck-fire he was up to.

It was while I was in this self-righteous and somewhat conceited state of chagrin, muttering under my breath, that I sensed a presence in the rocks off to my left. I stopped and saw it then, a heavy-set tawny brown mountain lion, or puma. It stood perched on a large boulder, some thirty yards away and slightly above me. Its dark eyes were fixed on me, and its white muzzle barely concealed the sharp teeth set within a slightly open mouth. I stood still, transfixed by its stare, feeling a little vulnerable, even intimidated, by my suddenly sensed solitude. I wasn't really scared. Their usual prey would include vicuña, rabbit, hare, and taruca or Andean deer. I had never heard of a puma attacking people, though I have since learned that there are records of such incidents in Argentina, some with mortal consequences. For the indigenous Quechuan people of Peru, the cougar represents Kay Pacha, the world of the living. Along with the condor, which represents the sky, and the snake, which represents the underworld, it constitutes a triadic symbol of the cosmos.

After only a few seconds, the giant cat turned aloofly and effortlessly sprang away into the rocks. I dumped my pack on the track, pulled out my camera from the lid pocket, and scrambled over towards the boulder where it had been standing, trying to get a second look without getting too close. But it had vanished.

Our arriero was visibly pleased to see me. He had kept himself occupied over the last two days collecting firewood, fishing for trout, checking on his burros and chewing lime and coca leaves. I was still excited about my puma and did my best to convey it. But despite his smiles and nodding, I'm not sure he understood. When at last Tony waltzed nonchalantly into camp a couple of hours later, I found a ready audience for my story. I told him about the puma, emphasizing the point that if only he had kept up, he would have seen it too. Tony listened with bemused patience. "Well," he said. "I saw some amazin' clouds, a real spectacle, like I've never seen before, nor likely will ever see again. If you hadn't been in such a blessed hurry to get down here, you would have seen them too." With our stories told and differences settled, we lit up our stove once again, set up the tent on the flat grass by the stream, and lay back to absorb the vista and ponder the regret of yet another unclimbed mountain.

The camp after we got lost on the wrong side of Urus Ridge, Peru 1989.

Lost on the wrong route on Nevado Toclaraju (6032m), Peru.

The roofed crevasse near our high camp on Toclaraju.

Quitaraju (6040m) seen from the bergschrund on the south-west face of Alpamayo.

Irrepressible Irish mountaineer, Tony Duboudin.

CHAPTER THIRTEEN
TERRORISTS IN HUARAZ

The months that I climbed in Peru coincided with the violent Tiananmen Square massacre in Beijing in June, 1989. It also coincided with the brutal peak of the revolutionary activity of the Maoist-inspired Shining Path or Sendero Luminoso movement in Peru. The group had been in operation for almost a decade executing highly organized guerilla warfare and violent terrorist activities throughout the country. In early 1989 the Australian Government was warning its citizens against travel to Peru. But I had been planning and training for 18 months, and I had no intention of cancelling or postponing my expedition.

Originally I had two goals that I wanted to accomplish in Peru. One was to climb Alpamayo's southwest face in the Cordillera Blanca. In this, I eventually succeeded. The other was to climb the west face of Yerupaja (6635m), Peru's second highest peak, in the neighbouring Cordillera Huayhuash. On arrival in Huaraz I learned however that the Huayhuash region was basically out of bounds due to hostile terrorist activity. Tourists were not allowed to travel there, and no locals were prepared to support any kind of climbing expedition in the region.

For the first six weeks or so of my two months in Peru, there were few signs of the Sendero. Mostly I was up in the mountains climbing, where the only people I and my team-mates encountered were either other climbers and trekkers, arrieros, or local Quechuan villagers and farmers. When we were back in Huaraz to recover between outings and buy supplies, their activity was a bit more noticeable. For example, every few days the power would go off in town for a half day or more. When asked what was causing the power outage, the local hotel or restaurant staff would invariably answer, "Terroristas! Sendero Luminoso." Apparently it was one of the terrorists' favourite tactics to blow up power lines up and down the valley. (It could of course have simply been the case that the local infrastructure was just falling to pieces, but no one mentioned that.)

One morning, while breakfasting on the famous 'Muesli Grande' at the restaurant next to the Casa de Guias, we heard from some newly arrived British climbers that a Welsh trekker had been murdered by Sendero Luminoso terrorists in the nearby Cordillera Huayhuash. He had been happened upon at night by a group of guerillas who had been raiding and looting the village of Olleras, dragged outside into the village plaza, tied to a park bench, subjected to a mock public trial and then executed. The British climbers had only recently read of the atrocity in their English newspapers. There had been no mention of it in the Peruvian media.[7]

News of the man's violent death certainly shook us up. It seemed clear that the Sendero Luminoso would target westerners, given the opportunity. It also confirmed the sense in the ban on climbing in the Huayhuash region, and on the need to take local advice seriously.

About a week later Tony, Val and I returned from our final climb together on Huascaran Sur (6747m), the highest mountain in Peru. Val and I had almost reached the summit, turning back only about thirty minutes short in worsening weather. On Tony's and my arrival back at our lodgings in Huaraz, the Hotel Colonial, we were informed by its owner Carlos that a night-time curfew had been imposed on account of a new threat of impending attack by the Sendero. To this was added the rumour that gringos were especially in danger, and that a full daytime curfew was not off the cards. With this possibility in mind, we spent the next day buying food supplies so we could cook for ourselves in the hotel common kitchen for as long as we needed. Sure enough, as the afternoon wore on we were informed that the next day was to be a full curfew. Nobody, especially gringos, was to be out and about in the town. The Sendero were planning an attack, probably at one of the popular

---

[7] His name was Edward Bartley, aged 24.

restaurants frequented by western climbers and trekkers. None of the restaurateurs wanted to take the risk of being targeted, and so were planning on staying shut.

Before the sun had fallen, Tony and I decided to get word out to our climbing contacts around Huaraz to come around to our hotel first thing in the morning for an all-day pancake party. We had bought plenty of ingredients, and just needed someone to bring the necessary beverages. The weather looked to be clear and sunny and our hotel had a sizeable rear courtyard, surrounded by a high brick wall. It was the perfect setting to sit out the enforced lockdown.

By ten o'clock the next morning we had a good little crowd of revelers. Kiwi Lionel Clay and Brit Pete Sykes, fresh back from a difficult new route on Taulliraju's formidable south face, had brought along a box of beer. Val arrived with Jorque and a bottle of maple syrup from her luxury cache of specially imported trekking expedition supplies. A number of welcome new faces appeared, climbers we had not yet met but who had heard about the party and didn't want to miss out. The only music we could find was a Fleetwood Mac album, which we played over and over on a battered tape recorder powered by two raw wires stuffed into a wall socket.

By nightfall it began to dawn on us that our party-makers all had to head home to their own places of accommodation. Val and Jorque had sensibly left before sunset, but most others had been too lost in the card-playing or dancing or culinary delights to consider the problems posed by the night-time curfew. We took our problem to Carlos, who had had too much to drink. He suggested that he, Tony and I should all escort the guests home to their respective hotels. There would be safety in numbers, he thought.

It was eerily quiet on the streets. Normally the town would be alive and thronging at night, with colourful street stalls and food vans and musicians, children playing, dogs fighting, men drinking. Instead it was dark and ominous, with shadowy figures disappearing down alley ways, the occasional dog barking or trotting off towards the river. By the time we had dropped off the last pair of guests at their hotel, it was about nine p.m., and the three of us made a bee-line down the main street past the Plaza de Armas in the direction of Carlos's hotel. Suddenly out of nowhere we heard the roar of a diesel engine. An armoured truck lurched towards us, blinding us with its spot-lights. Tearing along either side of the truck appeared about a dozen soldiers armed with sub-machine guns. Stopped in our tracks, we were quickly surrounded by balaclava-hooded soldiers thrusting their black glistening weapons at us and barking commands of "Manos arriba! Manos arriba!" At first we hesitated, stunned with disbelief and bewilderment at what was happening. But the metallic ratcheting of weapons being cocked prompted us to obey, along with the sense that these young soldiers, wound up tight in expectation of a

Sendero terrorist attack, were on a knife's edge. For a few tense moments confusion reigned, with our appealing cries of "touristas" being confused for "terroristas," and the drunken Carlos fumbling with his ID papers. I grimaced and braced my body, waiting for the shock of hot lead to rip into my flesh, committing my life to God in silent prayer. But Carlos, urgently pleading with the commander, managed to calm things down, and soon the cordon stepped back, allowing us to lower our hands, trembling with adrenaline-induced fear and relief.

On our way home, following a harsh reprimand from the commander, Carlos explained in slurred and broken English what had happened. That afternoon the military had received intelligence of a planned bombing attack, and had been lying in wait to intercept the terrorists. When they had seen our dark figures walking down the street, they immediately assumed the worst and launched their offensive. We had been lucky: quite likely they had been high on coca and primed for action. Thankfully Carlos had been able to mediate for us his gringo friends, assuring the soldiers that we were no threat and were on our way home.

Back at the hotel the electricity was out again. I wrote in my diary by candlelight, still tense and alert and unable to relax. In the bed on the other side of the room Tony's body lay inert, a rhythmic snoring the only sign of life. I envied his ability to sleep anywhere, anytime. We had faced many dangers in the mountains together and survived. How ironic it would have been, right at the end of our adventures, to have been shot dead in downtown Huaraz, branded as curfew breakers and foreign collaborators with the Sendero Luminoso.

Val Pitkethly with local alpine guide Jorque, Cordillera Blanca, Peru (1989).

Adam leaving the bivvy on the glacier below Alpamayo, first attempt. This was just after the death of a Swiss climber on the French Direct route.

CHAPTER FOURTEEN
TRAGIC DEATHS

I haven't known many climbers personally who have died climbing. Anton Wopereis is one. Anton was 54 years old when he was killed on New Years' Day in 2008 after a sixty metre fall near the summit of Mt Cook with a client. Details are sketchy, but the coroner's report suggests an unprotected fall triggered by a soft snow slide. I remember Anton for his enormous, tireless strides through deep fresh snow on Lake Louise, for demonstrating the method of hanging on your ice tools to place a screw, and for his personal encouragement to me to take on big alpine ice routes. His slides of Alpamayo inspired my own decision to head to Peru. When I first gazed upon the sheer and sinister north faces of the Argentière valley from the Aiguille Tour in France, I remembered Anton's pictures of climbing unroped by torchlight up the first few thousand feet of seventy degree ice on Les Droites.

Adelaide climber Mark Auricht was another. Mark died from some kind of cerebral hemorrhage or oedema on Everest in 2001 at the age of 37. He had made the first Australian ascent of Makalu with David Hume in 1995. I never climbed with Mark, but had enjoyed numerous conversations about his trips and plans. For his trip to Ama Dablam in 1989 I gave Mark a pair of strap-on crampons. I like to think I encouraged him in his love for the mountains.

Colin Reece was one of the leading pioneers of crag climbing in Adelaide from the early 1970s. He was known throughout the country. He was killed in 2010 in a fall at Robin Falls in the Northern Territory. Climbing blogs were soon filled with tributes after news spread of his death. One contributor to Chockstone said this about Colin:

> He was one of those rare breeds of people who has achieved great things but yet remained humble. Despite putting up huge numbers of new routes (including a significant number of great classics), he was prepared to climb with anyone regardless of their climbing ability. Many a beginner over the years has enjoyed his mentoring, encouragement and absolute passion for climbing. You could not find a more genuine person. He was a great guy and his tragic death is an enormous loss to his friends and the climbing world in general.

That also captures my experience of Colin, and although I have heard it said that he was a bit odd, he never seemed so to me. He took me under his wing when I was just 17 and only a year into climbing. I met Colin either at Morialta or at the outdoor shop I was working in at the time, I can't remember which. He arranged to pick me up from home one Saturday morning in his clapped-out Datsun 180B to go climbing. I struggled to find a place for my big feet amid all the ropes, slings, drinking bottles, and climbing hardware piled up in the footwell. The wheel bearings on that car were shot and once it passed 40 kph the already rattly engine was accompanied by a loud whirring from the front wheels, making conversation nigh on impossible.

Colin had climbed pretty much every line worth climbing in South Australia, so keeping him interested was a challenge. Mostly we just bumbled around at Morialta, but once we hiked up a creek near Waterfall Gully, pushing our way through thick bush and blackberry thorns to what Colin believed was a virgin unclimbed cliff. It was only about eight to ten metres tall, but Colin put up two little routes, naming the better of them *Lawn Green* (12).

Many people are tempted to ameliorate the pain when faced with tragic loss by saying something like: at least he died doing what he loved. I dislike that saying used of climbing deaths. They did not die doing what they loved. They died falling, freezing, out of control, broken, afraid. I remember when news broke of Ueli Steck's fall to his death on Nuptse in 2017. I recalled his saying somewhere that dying in the mountains was the one thing he wanted to avoid. "I don't have a death wish", he wrote in 2010. "On the contrary, I am hanging on to my life like never before." The grim reality is that he didn't die doing what he loved. He died falling, sliding, bouncing, out of control. I would never wish such an end on anyone. In his book *Lament for a Son*, written after his son Eric's climbing death in Austria, philosopher Nicholas Wolterstorff reflected on the irrationality of death and the inability to fit tragic loss into a meaningful, coherent narrative. "There's a hole in the world now," he writes. "In the place where he was, there's now just nothing.... There's nobody now who saw just what he saw, knows what he knew, remembers what he remembered, loves what he loved.... My son is gone. Only a hole remains."

It's difficult to conceptualize the passing of these men I knew. Imagining their deaths is too terrible. But for me, somewhat removed from the loss experienced by people closer to them, there is more than just a hole left where they once were. Even though they are gone, they are part of my memory, and, through my experiences of them, in some way part of me. I believe they were outstanding climbers and remarkable human beings. Who was I that they befriended me? I certainly feel that I received from them way more than I could ever have given. Yet they were gracious enough to receive the little admiration, respect, and youthful company that I could offer, not to mention the odd belay. May they rest in peace.

CHAPTER FIFTEEN

DIAMOND COULOIR FAIL

One afternoon in September of 1990 Paul Horne and I arrived at the oft-used bivouac rock at the base of the Diamond Couloir route on Mt Kenya (5199m). The Diamond Couloir is, or was, a 2000 foot-long icicle just ten miles south of the equator. Today, with global warming and glaciers receding all over the world, it is pretty much non-existent. In 1990 it was fully formed, but only just. Together with my brother Michael, who had made the trek in from Chogoria with us and had settled in to Mackinders Hut to watch our ascent, we had officially named ourselves the first ever All Australian Diamond Couloir Expedition, although we were well aware that one or two other Aussies, including Everest summiteer Greg Mortimer, had already climbed it in multi-national teams.

Seven days had passed since we had organized a driver with "four-wheel drive transport" to take us from Nairobi to the start of the approach walk at the Mt Kenya Bandas at 10,000 feet. What turned up at our hotel was a tiny beaten up Suzuki Jimny. My research since suggests that it was probably a 1984 SJ410, assembled in Nairobi. Its puny one litre engine was built to produce a maximum 45 brake horsepower. The specimen standing before us, hammered by years of abuse, looked like it might just manage 30. With its load of three big passengers and two weeks' worth of climbing gear, food and supplies, the little Suzuki laboured valiantly along the highway as far as Chogoria, but struggled up the last ten kilometres through the bamboo forest to the road end. Its low range drive-train options made no difference. If we hadn't hopped out to push it up the steeper sections, engine screaming and clutch melting, we would never have made it.

I remember how magical the landscape appeared as we made the walk in up the Gorges Valley to Simba Col, up and back to Point Lenana (4985m), then down to the Teleki Valley with the hyraxes. As children Mike and I had lived with our family in Tanzania at the foot of Mt Kilimanjaro and Mawenzi, and the same dreamy sense of enchantment and mystery took hold of me here in the alpine moonscape above the forest. At the Bandas we had spied an elephant in the cool glades at the forest edge, monkeys frolicking in the bamboo tree tops, and had heard a leopard coughing at night. There we had also employed two porters to help carry our kit and show us the way. At certain stages both Paul and Michael fell ill with altitude sickness, decorating the ground with their vomit and humouring the porters, but both were well by the time we arrived at Mackinders Hut. The Point Lenana ascent made for excellent acclimatization, although it was marred by the discovery of a recently dead Sykes' monkey, its frozen corpse curled up on the rocks near the Austrian Hut (4790m). One of our porters told us it had been deliberately lured by some trekkers up the mountain with biscuits and left to die in desolation from the altitude and cold.

Surveying the route from our bivouac, I felt both hopeful and uneasy. Hopeful, because here we were at last, after all the long months of planning and preparation. Uneasy, because it was unseasonably warm, and even here at just over 4000 metres, the little snow left among the rocks was melting and there was no night-time freeze. Depending on what we found, Paul and I accepted that we might be forced to forego the Diamond Couloir and try the Ice Window route to the right instead. Around four a.m. we set off by headlight towards the icefield at the base of the route, having stashed our bivouac kit under the boulder and taking only our climbing gear, water, and a little food.

Paul was ahead, clanging and tinkling over the dark volcanic rocks with his snow stakes and screws, pausing to put on crampons to head up the easy ice of the lower icefield. By the time I arrived he was ready to move. It felt great to strap on crampons again and kick up the frozen slope, the first time for me since Peru fifteen months before. Since then I had become engaged, and on the approach I had become conscious of a new, unsettling feeling inside, a homeward tug on my heart, with constant thoughts of my beloved fiancé and of her thoughts of me: her worry, her fear, her longing, her simultaneous anticipation and dread of news. Looking up at the dark towering precipice of rock and ice above, I suddenly felt out of place, like I didn't belong. Michael too had just become engaged, and Paul had only recently married, and I wondered if they felt the same. What had once been a singular devotion to and unalloyed love for the mountains had now been divided and dispersed. I had something else, some*one* else, to think about and live for now, and the whole "climbing thing" had suffered demotion in my priorities, losing its once lofty pride of place.

Nearing the base of the couloir proper, Paul's clanging stopped and I saw his headlight beam searching around to set up a belay. While I continued up towards him, the sudden sound of a big rock rushing past and then impacting with ice close by froze all movement. "Holy shit!" I called out. "Did you hear that?" Just then we heard and felt it again. I sank my tools into the ice and huddled my body into a tight, cowering ball, expecting more. After a few seconds of silence, I shouted out to Paul again. "Was that rock or ice?" In the dark we had seen nothing, and I felt suddenly vulnerable and exposed. "Don't know.

Sounded like a rock. Or an ice-block. Sounded big," called Paul.

Moments passed, while we each sat tight and silently thought through our options. I didn't feel at all confident. I wanted down, though was embarrassed to say so. My motivation had already been diminished by my new state of mind, and now, with this invisible threat and the possibility of imminent rock fall or ice collapse, I just wanted to be off the mountain, out of harm's way. I realised however that Paul might want otherwise. Compared to me he was a seasoned veteran, and I trusted his superior intuition and judgement when it came to assessing mountain hazards. I understood also that our climbing partnership constituted a mutual commitment according to which neither of us could just act unilaterally or arbitrarily. If Paul was bent on pressing on, in the absence of any objective evidence of disproportionate risk I would be bound to continue.

"What do you reckon?" Paul's reasoned voice had a calming effect. We had come such a long way and now the Diamond Couloir was within reach, right in front of us. I was eager not to let Paul down, eager too not to appear a coward, but here he was, inviting me to share my doubts. The dangers of rock strike would lessen as we got up into steeper territory, but once we were into the difficulties, it would be awkward to retreat if one of us did get hit. There was no helicopter rescue system here. It was now or never. "I don't feel good about it Paul", I admitted. "It's much too warm. If anything comes off from higher up, we're gonna get it."

Paul hesitated briefly before his terse reply. "Ok! I'll come down." The night had passed by the time we reached the bivouac boulder. We cast our eyes back on the route, now illuminated in the brightening sky. There was no sign of rock or ice fall, no scars in the snow cone, no large rocks lodged its dirty glacial surface. Had we imagined it? If Paul felt any disappointment, he never revealed it. As we made our way down the mountain, right until we returned and parted ways in Nairobi, he remained entirely gracious toward me, even supportive of my judgement, and his generosity built up in me the belief that we had made the right decision. And in fact, my fears were not altogether without foundation. I later read about the terrifying ice avalanche witnessed by Rob Taylor the day after he and Henry Barber climbed the Diamond Couloir back in 1978:

> A fallen icicle, a tumbling stone, it is sudden; no one sees how it starts. The entire face lets loose, a hundred thousand tons of snow. It roars and rumbles down from the Gate of Mists over the headwall ad into the Couloir, finally spilling onto the talis slope at the bottom at over 150 miles an hour. The noise is deafening. It lasts maybe thirty seconds. But in that

time the entire South Face is scoured clean – down to bedrock and black ice. Not a patch of snow remains.[8]

Looking back today, however, I am not so sure. Perhaps it was just another lost opportunity. Another failure of nerve in the face of threat. Another fail in a long litany of climbing fails. From one perspective, what happened on Mt Kenya those thirty years ago could be interpreted as a kind of emblematic paradigm of a whole series of personal failures that have marked my life, of crises where - overwhelmed by fears, real or imagined, or divided inside - I have avoided, rather than pushed through, the challenge before me. Many people would try to console me here. At least you're alive, they would say. At least you weren't pulverized by a chunk of hurtling ice or rock. And true enough, the expedition was far from wasted. Combined with a nostalgic visit back to our childhood home in Moshi beneath Kilimanjaro and a week swimming, snorkeling, and fishing on the Mombasa coast, the entire adventure forged between me and my brother Michael a special bond which abides to this day. But what is life, what is brotherhood, without courage and integrity? What is friendship and adventure without shared, unwavering fidelity to a transcendent, all-consuming purpose? I don't want to allow past failures

---

[8] Rob Taylor, *The Breach: Kilimanjaro and the Conquest of Self* (New York: Coward, McCann and Geoghegan, 1981), 85.

and dubious decisions to obscure the many gifts, achievements, and successful adventures that grace my life. Yet the Diamond Couloir stands forever in my mind as an ambivalent witness: to my passion, drive, and ambition on the one hand; and to my doubt, weakness, and fear on the other, both as a climber, and as a man.

Mt Kenya and the Diamond Couloir from Mackinders' Hut. My brother Michael and Paul Horne in the foreground.

CHAPTER SIXTEEN
FALL ON CENTRE POST DIRECT

My first foray on Scottish ice nearly ended in death. It was January in the year 2000. I had now been married almost a decade, our son was eight, and we had learned to live hand to mouth while I had been studying for church ministry. There had been no time, or money, for climbing. At some point during my seminary course I was invited to undertake further theological research on a scholarship, so in 1999 we moved from Adelaide to the picturesque city of Durham in the north of England for me to pursue a PhD at the university's theology school in the shadow of Durham's famous 1000 year-old cathedral. We had been in Durham for about four months and were reveling in its winter. Among the reasons I had chosen Durham for further study was its dual proximity to the beautiful Lake District fells and to wild Scottish ice. The university had its own mountaineering club, and I soon learned they were arranging a trip to Creagh Meagaidh in central Scotland. They were looking for an older driver for their rented sixteen-seater bus, someone who would qualify for better insurance rates. When I volunteered, they were quick to bag my services. I was about a decade older than most of them, and as I steered the bus full of young climbers northwards along the cold dark roads, they regarded me with a certain awe as I shared tit-bits of my experiences of climbing around the world.

As far as my knowledge of Scottish ice crags go, I had heard of Glencoe, the Cairngorms, and of course Ben Nevis. These were the famed play-grounds of such old-time, hard-core mountaineers as Hamish McInnes, Tom Patey, and Rusty Baillie. But Creagh Meagaidh was unknown to me, and having never bothered to consult any guidebooks prior to our departure on that Friday evening, I wasn't expecting anything impressive. I was still none the wiser as we made our midnight trek in up the valley from the Aberarder Farm carpark in light snow. Clouds and light snow obscured any view, and we hastily pitched our tents to get out of the increasingly blustery wind. By 3am it was blowing a gale, and I spent the rest of the night struggling to keep the nylon ceiling of the tent, blown flat across my face, from suffocating me. When in the chill, cold light of dawn I emerged from the bent and battered frame of my new Vango tent, I finally took in my first view of the wide corrie of iced up cliffs and gullies that make up Creagh Meagaidh.

I gazed up at the dark iced-up faces, searching for possible climbs. I was immediately struck by a steep, straight central line that divided the main north-east face into two. A narrow snow couloir over 1000 feet long, with a steepish couple of pitches about two thirds up before the exit gully, it presented the most obvious and most attractive route to the top of the giant crag. I had always read that Scottish ice was the worst: sugary, bottomless vertical snow; chossy broken rock; verglassed edges and steps; moss-filled cracks; spindrift avalanches; bad weather; white-outs, and so on. But here I was, staring up at what appeared to be a perfect alpine couloir, but with easy access and straightforward descent. After a stormy night, the sky was clear and the temperature comfortably below zero. It seemed like a no-brainer. I had been teamed up with two younger climbers, Dave and Wilkie, and as we brewed up and organized our gear, they asked what I wanted to climb. Without hesitation I pointed up to my line. "What about that?" I asked. "Looks absolutely perfect."

"Oh, wow! Ok. That's Centre Post Direct. About Grade 5," Dave replied. He sounded nervous.

"What do you reckon?" I inquired. "Looks like a perfect line. First 800 feet looks like just an easy snow slope. We can rope up and belay for the steep pitches if you like. Then an easy exit out to the top. Looks very doable. How do you get down from these climbs? Walk out the back across the plateau and down that big gully to the left?"

I was somewhat surprised, even bemused by their hesitation. They had assured me that between them they had accumulated several years' alpine climbing experience in Scotland and Europe, and apparently Dave was well accomplished on rock. For someone like me, schooled in the mountains of New Zealand and the waterfalls of Canada, the route appeared fairly benign. Unwisely, the fact that I hadn't climbed with either of these young men before, not to mention that I hadn't worn crampons or done any alpine climbing since embarking on marriage and family life ten years ago, didn't enter into my assessment of the suitability of the route.

After a sluggish and late state, the first 700 feet or so passed like a breeze. The initial snow ramp of about 40 degrees gradually steepened to 60 degrees, and the first few hundred feet of soft snow gave way to firmer and more consolidated snow-ice as we climbed. I had persuaded them to move unroped with me, to trust good axe placements and maintain three points of contact. I felt invigorated, alive and entirely at home on this familiar ground, thrilled to be climbing once again after such a long lay-off. The view across the crags and down to Lochan a' Choire and the snowy Coire Ardair valley was enthralling, and the speedy gain in height and exposure lent the route the sense of a truly alpine endeavour.

Around 11 a.m. we arrived at the base of a steep wall of ice, kicking narrow stances and tying off on a sling girth-hitched around a thickish free icicle solidly fastened to the ice above and below it. Searching around it soon became obvious to me that hopes of a solid ice-screw placement would be vain. While the snow we had climbed and were standing on was hard, the ice of the wall before and above us was mush, and to the right it was already weeping with the daytime rise in temperature. The icicle we were tied into looked pretty solid, but it was only about 6 inches in diameter, and its base wasn't broad enough to safely accept a screw, which would probably weaken the icicle anyhow. The idea of all three of us being tied into a single point was unnerving, and I liked even less the thought of relying on it to lead a steep pitch of bad ice. While Wilkie scratched around trying to find a rock placement, Dave and I munched on sandwiches and consulted about the route ahead.

"So, do you want to lead?" he asked.

"Hmm, not really. I don't like the look of that wall to be honest." I craned my neck back to survey the pitch. "There's at least a good 100 feet of steep climbing on pretty mushy ice. There won't be any pro, and the belay is far from ideal. I'm certainly not confident to tackle it."

"Well I'm willing to give it a go if you like," said Dave. I was surprised. "You sure? It's no problem for us to back off. No point in taking any big risks. There's always tomorrow. I've had a lot of fun already." I turned to

Wilkie for his opinion. He had managed to push a small nut into a manky-looking crack for the kind of anchor that amounts at best to a psychological sedative, or at worst, to a false sense of security. He had the rope nicely laid out over his feet and was hitched up and ready to belay. "Not me," he announced. "If Dave wants to try it, that's fine with me. Otherwise I've had a cracking morning out. We can go down and do something else later today, or wait 'til tomorrow."

Dave's sudden confidence, after his hesitation earlier in the day, might have been encouraging in better circumstances. "Yeah, I'll give it a crack. Can always come down if it looks dicey." But as he geared himself up to lead the mushy ice-wall I felt decidedly uneasy. While we had been stuffing around, a thick blanket of cloud had formed in the upper valley and risen to envelope us. It was definitely warmer than when we had started out. And the ice wall, which wasn't well formed to begin with, was literally liquefying before our eyes. Dave's first tentative moves out from our belay stance, with Wilkie belaying, only heightened my anxiety. Raking desperately at the ice with his tools, and kicking blindly with his front points, he shakily moved upwards. He was hardly the example of balanced, precise ice climbing. At about 20 feet out he tried to place a screw, pushing it into the mush with his left hand while trembling precariously on his boots. But no sooner had he clipped into it than it pulled out and slid down the rope. Moving up further, he kept thrashing his boots into the mush, keeping his heels too high and never gaining any sort of secure footing. When he was up about 25 feet, his axe swings became increasingly ineffective and unsteady, and I began to think I should say something. Was he pushing on to make an impression? He really looked like he might fall at any moment. It was becoming too agonizing to look on in silence. "Hey Dave, it doesn't look that great," I called out. "Why don't you come down and we'll call it a day?"

"Yeah, I think I'm going to come down. Watch me here...." And with those words, Dave peeled off backwards. His tools didn't seem to rake out or pop. It was more like he just let go. By the time he reached me, perched on my narrow snow step directly in his fall line, he was a dead weight flying upside-down. Although he only glanced me, the impact felt like I'd been hit by a truck. I was knocked down and felt the rope jerk tight on my harness, my vision momentarily darkened and my breath gone. Dave's body hurtled on past, bouncing once on the angled snow just below us then disappearing from view. He must have travelled 60 feet by the time the rope took his weight, and Wilkie, catching some of the force of the fall on his belay device attached to his harness, was ripped off his stance. Glancing up in bewildered panic, I saw that Wilkie's feel-good anchor had predictably pulled, leaving all three of us hanging from the single sling tied off around the icicle.

It took a moment to regain both our senses and our feet. With our stances recovered, our combined weight came off the anchor, but the live rope still pulled hard and tight downwards out of sight, and there was no movement nor any response to our loud shouts to indicate whether Dave was even conscious. At last the rope stirred and the strain eased somewhat, and finally we heard Dave's forlorn voice calling from below. He was okay, he said. Or at least he thought so. He was bleeding from his face, but apparently had no broken bones or serious injuries. I urged him to make himself safe, to kick a stance and anchor into his ice tools, which he still had strapped to his wrists. In the meantime Wilkie and I had to re-sort the ropes so I could belay him down to Dave. With the fall I suddenly felt responsible to get these young men down safely, and felt obliged by my seniority - perhaps a little paternalistically - to belay them down pitch by pitch and leave the less protected downclimbing to myself. We were still uncertain of how Dave had pulled up, whether he was in shock, how bad his bleeding was and so on. It was only around 1 p.m., but we were 700 feet up and needed to get down without further mishap.

After belaying Wilkie down to Dave, with instructions for him to set up a solid belay with a snow stake or two, I got myself ready for Wilkie's belay call, before dismantling the anchor. The girth hitched sling had cut in and refrozen into the wet ice, and was impossible to remove without damaging the icicle, so I left it behind and began the descent. Thankfully we found that Dave's bleeding from a cut on his forehead had stopped, and by the time I reached them he had gathered his wits and appeared chirpy and prepared for the downclimb. My insistence that we belay the entire descent was happily accepted, but it did mean that what had taken us only a couple of hours to ascend would take at least three times as long to descend. From each stance, I would belay first Wilkie and then Dave down a full 50 metres. Then they would belay me down to them, and we would repeat the movement. It was slow work. Dave moved laboriously and unsteadily, and Wilkie seemed to take ages each pitch to secure a belay. I was spending at least an hour at every belay point, often more: paying out slack, waiting, paying out again, waiting again, thirstily sucking on snowballs, shifting weight, bracing my back to the rising wind. It was straightforward climbing, the even couloir only interrupted by a steep rocky step lower down that we needed to bypass to the right. But at this latitude it fell dark by 3 p.m. and the temperature plummeted. Spindrift began to cascade down the couloir in endless waves, only to be whipped back upwards in wild wind gusts. I was having trouble with my headlight, which kept slipping off my helmet, and my jacket hood kept ripping off in the wind allowing washes of spindrift to gush untrammeled into my exposed neck. I felt cold, thirsty, hungry, and fatigued. I began to realise how physically unprepared I was for the demands of the downclimb, how a decade of sedentary life had sapped my stamina and conditioning, and by the time we reached the easier ground near the base of the snow ramp around 8 p.m., I was shattered.

Half an hour later we plodded back to the ring of tents, arriving to a raucous welcome. With the hot drinks and soup came eager interrogation. Some had seen us high on the route before cloud had hidden us from view. What had happened? Why so late back down? Had we climbed the ice wall? Had something gone wrong? As news of Dave's fall got around, fits of laughter began to break out. I was appalled. We had all nearly been killed. Didn't he know the basic rule of alpine climbing: do not fall? This ain't no indoor gym. This is a freaking mountain. This is ice climbing. As I railed through these interior objections, I suddenly realized how angry I was, how I had suppressed my fury on the climb for the sake of safety, getting us down, shepherding the lads home to safety. Who did this Dave think he was, putting us through such risk? How dare he climb to the very edge of his capacity, beyond it even, without a care for his colleagues and the potentially deadly impact of his failure?

But still they laughed and chuckled. "Tell you what Dave," one young lad piped up in a thick Yorkshire accent. "How 'bout tomorrow we take you up to the pinnacle atop Raeburn's Gully, tie one end of the rope to a massive big belay and let you throw yourself off for a huge fookin' winger." I began to catch on. Apparently Dave was infamous for falling off stuff, including ice climbs. To them our mishap was a 'here we go again' event, and I a fool caught up in someone else's gamble. I had been duped, that was all. My anger evaporated. I was too exhausted to nurse it further. After slaking my thirst and filling my belly, I crawled into my broken tent, and lay there in my sleeping bag, trying to sleep, but unable to get away from imagining the scenario had the anchor failed, had Dave broken his leg or neck, had I been skewered by his ice tools or crampons when he crashed past me. I felt the nervous tension in my body and clenched fists as I saw in my mind's eye our three bodies bouncing and sliding down the couloir, smashed and broken and lifeless as rag dolls. Tears rolled down into my ears as I thought of my family, and I thanked God that we had instead survived and got down safely, vowing never again to take on such a serious undertaking with a stranger. I had a wife. I had a son. I was an ordained minister with a vocation to serve others. My days of youthful carelessness had to be over.

Creag Meagaidh cloaked in winter dress, seen from the approach track up the Coire Ardair valley. The Centre Post Direct route follows the longest, most direct, vertical ice line in the centre of the main buttress, just right of centre in the photo. It is known for punishing the unwary with big leader falls.

CHAPTER SEVENTEEN

NO PICNIC ON MONT BLANC: PART I

Anyone who says the *via normale* on Mont Blanc is a waltz deserves a whipping. Maybe in late August when the snow has all melted back to 12,000 feet and the Gouter Ridge is bare; maybe when the weather is sunny and warm and windless; maybe when the last 1000 feet up the Bosses Ridge is scoured by a two yard-wide crampon track. True, on a clear day from the Chamonix Valley Mont Blanc looks like a giant, benign ice-cream cone, an ideal spot for a lazy afternoon sledging with the kids.

But in the near-winter conditions I found it in on my first ever visit to the French Alps, Mont Blanc is another matter. From Chamonix the keen eye, lingering a while on the 15,700 foot summit ridge, may chance to spot streams of spindrift blasting into Italy, the waxing and waning of smooth hogsback clouds – a sure sign of high winds, and the football field-sized patches of rock-hard bare ice glistening through the snow. As many die in this range each year as have ever lost their lives on Alaska's McKinley in the whole of its climbing history. I've heard the mortality rate has reached as high as one a day through the high season. 'Death Gully' on the Grand Couloir of the Gouter Ridge is no exception: it has become the specialized research focus of mountain accidentality.[9] It is no place for a picnic. Underestimate this baby, and it will likely eat you.

Our Mont Blanc expedition in 2001 was at least six months in the making. After the accident in Scotland I had vowed to myself not to do anything too serious in the hills any more. But the opportunity to climb Mont Blanc was not something I could easily pass up. It held out to me the chance to realize a long-held and seemingly impossible mountaineering dream. Gaston Rébuffat's sublime prose and stunning photos in his *100 Climbs in the Mont Blanc Massif* had, ever since it was given me by my eldest brother for my 15th birthday, long captured my spellbound attention. But now I was over from Australia for three years with my family to study in England's north, and over the last six months the dreams had started to come together to form a real plan. My new climbing

---

[9] See Jacques Mourey et al., 'Accidentology of the Normal Route up Mont Blanc between 1990 and 2017' (May, 2018). On page 3 the authors report: "Between 1990 and 2011, 291 people were the subject of rescue operations between the Tete Rousse refuge (3,187 m) and the Gouter refuge (3,830 m). The severity rate was extremely high: 74 people were killed and 180 injured."

partner Eric and I had agreed on going together and so set a date early in the climbing season to avoid the crowds and thunderstorms of July and August. Then we headed to the Cairngorms twice through winter and twice to the Lake District in order to get to know one another better and practise working together on snow and ice. We enjoyed some very successful trips and got on well to boot.

Climbing with Eric proved redemptive for my climbing ambitions after the near disaster in Scotland with Dave and Wilkie. A good ten years older than I, Eric had loved nature and the outdoors from his early youth. He can name countless kinds of birds and plants and stops often on a climb or descent to watch the sky or mountains or a little insect or flower or listen to a bird call or some such thing. His friends tease him for being a real toy shopper as far as climbing equipment goes. I remember his barely concealed pride and self-consciousness at buying two fancy curved ice tools only days after I had slung off at all the unnecessary gadgetry available for steep ice. Trying to admire his purchase, and at heart somewhat envious, I really had to work hard to hide my stupefaction when he pulled out the additional specially-designed stuff sac with embossed logo he had bought to hold them.

For a true outdoorsman Eric was a fastidious fellow in many respects. He can live off bread and cheese or noodles and fish for a fortnight at a time, yet unlike most climbers I know who are quite content to make do with the sanitary and domestic limitations imposed by life in the hills, Eric won't even touch say a cup of tea unless it comes in a carefully washed and rinsed cup, nor yet will he drink it with any milk but fresh pasteurized (no powdered or UHT thankyou very much!). And while he organizes his personal items and packing in minute and laborious detail, he often remains confused about where things are, sometimes misplacing or forgetting items of importance. He is notorious for taking ages to get ready – seeming constantly to be adjusting laces, zips, pack, belts, hats, glasses (different kinds for different light or temperature conditions). It became almost entertaining for me to observe the way he entered into an endless ritual in removing and replacing gloves at every belay point (all three sets!). On one climb at Corrie-an-Sneaichda in the Cairngorms he spent nearly an hour putting in a single piece of rock protection, the gloves coming off and on several times, only to have the piece fall out spontaneously as he started off climbing again - at which there issued from his lips a violent, screaming bawl. All the while I had been freezing my extremities on an eight-inch belay ledge in a roaring wind with regular waves of spindrift avalanches sweeping over me, not daring to shout at him or ask how things were going for fear of throwing his concentration, or worse, of copping his wrath – of which I have not yet knowingly, nor ever wish to be the object.

Could Eric be a clinical case of the true obsessive-compulsive climber? Perhaps. Yet he is a careful, skilled, and competent mountaineer - far more so than I - a natural in the hills with good judgement and balance. When many years later in the crazy hot season of 2015 we met in Chamonix for a month of climbing, I was happy to let Eric - by then in his 60s - do most of the leading, especially on more difficult pitches. And while he seems to take forever to sort himself out and will re-tie knots over and again to get them just right, his rope work is sound when operative. Whether he endures you or likes you, you can never be sure. But Eric and I understand each other and climb well and don't mind long spells of silence between us.

Eric invited along on the Mont Blanc trip three workmates, with one of whom in particular - Dan - Eric has spent many years climbing easy snow routes, winter scrambling, and walking and rock climbing in the fells. Dan's idea of a rewarding day in the hills is to hammer along a trail with a big pack for thirty miles or more. But his irritatingly high level of fitness is balanced by a lively humour and irrepressible culinary skills with a single pot and petrol stove. He also has a big car (by English standards), and so was needed to drive and fit all the gear. Then there were Paul and Kerry, a lovestruck couple relatively new to rock climbing but who have been keen walkers and serious outdoors-folk for ages. All five of us headed to Helvellyn in the Lake District for a snowy scramble to test crampons, boots and fitness. Yet nearing our departure to France I remained concerned that while all showed themselves to be strong winter scramblers, neither Paul nor Kerry had had much practice in basic snow and ice-techniques – right down to self-arresting with an ice-axe. In fact, I was the only one of the five who had spent time in glaciated terrain, knew about rope-work for glacier travel and crevasse rescue, and had much experience in lead climbing and various belay techniques (for a variety of abnormal situations - running belays, prussik self-belays, pulley rescue, multiple abseil descent, boot-axe soft snow belays, body belays, dynamic belays and so on), all of which are important alternative skills in out-of-the-ordinary conditions in the mountains. I guess I kind of trusted that the three non-climbers would recognize their own limitations. No doubt they would be able to enjoy some easier acclimatization climbs with Eric and me, but I believed they would be canny enough to know when to opt out if things got more technically demanding.

With busy schedules organization came late. A week before the due date of departure, Eric, Paul, Kerry and I headed out onto a local rugby field for me to try and teach them glacier travel and crevasse rescue in two hours flat. Dan was too busy to join us. Then at sunset we headed for Eric's to study maps and photos, and to draw up a gear list and game plan for the six days we would have in Chamonix. I emphasized the need for appropriate acclimatization, drawing on stories from my exploits in Peru and Africa. So did all the guidebooks and available route information. We were to spend Friday and Saturday travelling to Chamonix, too long in Eric's book, but more manageable for the two drivers, Dan and Paul. So we agreed days one and two – the Sunday and Monday - were to be spent perhaps up the Argentière Glacier climbing an easy snow-route on a mountain up to 13,000 feet, sleeping no higher than around 10,000 feet. By Monday night we would get to the Tete Rousse hut at 10,000 feet, established and in position at the bottom of the Gouter Ridge route on Mont Blanc. There we would also spend Tuesday night, perhaps with a short *recce* during the day to the base of the Gouter Ridge, especially to check out the infamous 'Bowling Alley' or 'Death Gully', the couloir crossing where many are killed every year by rockfall or avalanche. Only on Wednesday, after two nights at the Tete Rousse at 10,000 feet, would we ascend the 2000 foot west ridge of the Aiguille de Gouter to the Gouter hut at 12,523 feet, poised for the summit bid. That would leave Thursday to ascend the mountain and return all the way to Chamonix, quite the normal scenario for summit day in Mont Blanc climbing. Friday and Saturday would be buffer days in case of bad weather. On Sunday night we had to be back in Calais for the ferry.

Ideally you should spend a whole week doing two or three acclimatization climbs, spend two days recovering in the valley, and then only make for Mont Blanc or one of the other big 4000 metre peaks. Yet if I were to return to Chamonix tomorrow for another six days, I would still hold to the plan we drew up. It provides adequate acclimatization within the given constraints of time. 10,000 feet really is, I believe, the first major 'thresh-hold.' Only when one can sleep well at that height should one move on to sleep at the next stage, say, at 13,000 feet. It is not how high one goes during the day that counts so much as where one sleeps at night. Climb high, sleep low, is the old adage. Years before in Peru I had climbed an 18,000 feet peak with no noticeable ill-effect on only my fifth day in the country, simply by working progressively from three nights at 10,000 feet (with day-time sorties to between 11,000 and 15,500 feet), then one night at 13,800. From there we went to the summit and returned to 10,000 feet. A week after that I was climbing mountains to 20,000 feet with few altitude-related effects.

So, that was the plan. We popped the corks and drank to a safe and successful trip. The week crawled past until at last Friday morning arrived and we jammed into Dan's car and headed off – I somewhat quiet and contemplative, conscious of the fact that this was a serious undertaking and may eventuate in death for one or all of us, if not on the mountain then perhaps on the highway! On questioning Dan on his aspirations, he said he was only out for a good time in the hills, and if he could manage the Mont Blanc climb, he would consider it a bonus. Paul and Kerry too said they would simply be happy to get to one of the high huts. They had recently studied a video of the sharp and exposed summit ridge, and were apprehensive about their capabilities for such a venture.

I had been checking the weather forecasts on the internet. On my latest search I learned that it was to be a sloppy weekend in Chamonix, with improving weather from Monday right on into the week. That would work well for us. Conditions were perfect for road travel: cloudy and cool, yet a calm sea for the crossing - a blessing since Eric is hopelessly prone to travel-sickness, and even on the calm sea was queasy and paranoid about falling ill. He was hungry by then, Dan having polished off most of Eric's sandwiches on the drive down. I said some food in the belly would help, but Eric fairly enough detests fast food at the best of times and even more so when travelling, so he starved his way virtually all the way to Chamonix, bearing with sullen dignity a foodless night and morning in a village campsite in northern France.

There was no view of the mountains. We camped in a soggy field in the village of Argentière, five kilometres up valley from Chamonix. You could just make out the great icy tongues of the glaciers emerging from the misty heights and cascading down into the valley. For me it brought home memories of Westland New Zealand with the Fox and Franz Josef glaciers tumbling down to sea level. Here we were at 4,000 feet, but with nothing but continuous rain we could do no more than go shopping and enjoy 'carbing up' for when conditions would permit movement. I took the time to go to Mass in the beautiful church in Argentière and visit the cemetery with its many graves of alpine guides killed in the mountains. It was an emotional moment as I remembered my loved ones in the company of French-speaking saints.

It was perhaps this set-in rain and cloud that got Eric wondering whether we would get a chance at Mont Blanc at all. Rain down here spelled snow up there, and that would slow things down considerably. Plus, he'd been talking to some old salts from the Sunderland climbing club. They said Mont Blanc was a romp, that you should hang about for good weather – don't go out in it and get wet acclimatizing - and then just 'go for it' in a clear weather window. Here we were in Chamonix, the alpinist's Mecca, and the hours were ticking past with no let-up in sight. In a few days we'd have to pack our kit and head home. We should wait for a good forecast, say Monday night, then just go for it – straight to the top of Mont Blanc in a three-day push, forget the rest. At least, that was Eric's proposal.

Indeed, the weather looked set to improve late Monday. Tuesday was to be a bright start with cloud developing later, then Wednesday was to be the first of a series of clear days right through until Saturday, when thunderstorms were expected to develop. But that would be too late, thought Eric, and millions of people would be on the hill, wanting to do what we were doing. If we could be up at Tete Rousse on Monday night, then to the Gouter on Tuesday, we could summit on Wednesday and chill out for two days, maybe finishing up with some ice-bouldering on one of the glaciers.

Inside I wondered about all the acclimatization plans we had made. They had largely been my idea. On the way down through France I had studied the guidebook, and even had two easy route possibilities in mind – one on the Aiguille d'Argentière, the other on the Aiguille de Tour. Then there was the possibility of the beautiful Midi-Plan traverse. But they were my ideas, my way of wanting to squeeze every ounce of value out of these six short days, and since the others seemed to think Eric's proposal sounded good, I abandoned my acclimatization plans and capitulated happily enough. Some small doubt came in the form of a question from Kerry. She asked me if I thought it was pushing it – going straight onto Mont Blanc without acclimatization. Yes, I said, I think it is. It was bold, to be sure, but at least it was action, and so perhaps better than sitting around in the tents getting grumpy or else in Chamonix drinking expensive French espresso. Time would tell.

So we rang the huts, only just open for the season and managed by full-time staff. It is a system quite unlike anything I have known. The huts are like spartan hotels: they feed you, bed you, wake you, even give you hut slippers – all for a fee of course. One doesn't need a sleeping bag, or even a stove – so we were told. Just francs or plastic. It would mean light packs – day food, clothing, and climbing gear only. Our bookings went through okay.

We were going to beat the hordes. The French Alps are world-renowned for being hopelessly overcrowded. Gouter Hut swells with 200 a night through July and August, over half of whom fail to reach the summit. So the plan was underway. We were to drive down to Les Houches around lunchtime on Monday, telepherique up to Bellevue, cog-tram-car up to Nid d'Aigle at 8116 feet, and 'hike' to Tete Rousse – one and a half hours in the guidebooks. Then Tuesday was supposedly to be another 'easy' day – the ridge up to Gouter hut, a climb put at two and a half hours in the books. Then all going well, the summit on Wednesday.

Memorial stone in honour of guides killed in the mountains, in the church yard of L'église Saint-Pierre d'Argentiere in the Chamonix Valley.

CHAPTER EIGHTEEN
NO PICNIC ON MONT BLANC: PART II

We left the tents up at the Argentière campground, and handed in our passports to the campground manager, joking as we drove off that he would probably wait until we got around the corner before dismantling our campsite and hocking off our stuff at the local dealers: 'another group of Anglaises dogs destined to die in our mountains!' Those mountains were still invisible, hidden by a dense but progressively thinning layer of cloud. What would the queues be like for the telepherique? How low would the snow line be, and how much fresh snow would have fallen in these last three days? Would the sky clear for sunset? How would we fare at 8,000 feet for the walk up tonight? And tomorrow to 12,500 feet? Each of us had our questions.

But the telepherique station was quiet, and we the sole passengers on the cable car into the cold mist to Bellevue, just above the tree line. Patches of snow told us that it had been cold as low as this, and a cold sleet whipped up as we huddled at the lonely tram-way station for a long overdue train. It finally came some three hours late, by which time we had been joined by a Spanish threesome, equally equipped with bright goretex, plastic boots, and ice gear. The tram ground its way up and up, deeper into the white cloud, until at last it stopped suddenly where the line was abandoned at the outbreak of the first world war. Here already the snow was deep, the way obscured by mist and cloud. Four thirty p.m., and it began to snow. Pack on and waiting. Always waiting. Eric fiddling around with his pack, putting on or taking off layers, not content to make do with being a little warm or a little cold, adjusting his water-container on the outside of his pack, supposedly so he can get at it without taking his pack off, but always having to ask someone else to get it for him anyway since he can't reach it with all his gear on. I'm keen to head off. The Spaniards seem to be delaying, to let us go ahead and break trail. Finally we're off, and I set a slow, mechanical pace in the deep, soft snow, slipping here and there in the melt. It's puffing work. Sweat starts, snow falls, goggles mist up and just making out some descent tracks which I trust go the right way. I have memorized the map and the others follow silently like lambs.

Dan takes over the lead. Two hours go by and the Spaniards have passed us. The track has now joined the ridge which has steepened. We pass a cross marking the spot where some soul has fallen or frozen, and I inadvertently reach out for it for a handhold before I realize what it is. *Kyrie eleison*. Ice axes out and hands needed every few steps. Plenty of exposed scrambling, and finally quite a steep section of ice and snow on rock. The Spaniards are still on it, and have the rope on. Do you want the rope, they cry? I know I would: *Si, muchas gracias*! So a quick bowline around the waist and I'm off. Eric, more confident on this kind of ground, follows unroped, and by the time he's up I've rigged up our own line for Dan, Paul and Kerry. It takes a little while, but it protects the exposed section where a fall would be dangerous or possibly fatal.

With the breeze up, the mist clears for a moment and we can look up and down the ridge. Below us trail our tracks in the snow and far below, the tramline. Up we can see the Tete Rousse Glacier and across it, flashing bright in the evening sunlight, the hut. Less than an hour to go. It is hard work. What *do* I have in this rucsac? The mist closes again but we are oriented and Eric leads the final thrash across the snow-field to the hut. Bedlam in the foyer, a dangerously exposed ramp to the 'toilet' (straight through a hole in the floor of the outhouse onto the glacier – streams of used toilet paper billow into the air in gusts and whirlwinds), and temperature well below freezing now. Kerry has a headache, but we are happy to be here and on the way at last. Yet here also we learn for the first time that the huts have no supply of water. You have to buy it at two and a half quid for a litre and a half, and we know it will take at least three litres each to bring us back to hydration just for the last few hours of effort! I kick myself for leaving the stove and pots. I had felt naked heading off without them – they are my lifeline and first aid kit above the snowline – the only means of staying alive, melting snow for heat and water. So we pay up and drink and await our hut meal.

Eric is eating alone. He is happy (he says) to live on bread, cheese, and *saucisson sec* for three days, three meals a day. Our round one comes as a steaming bowl of soup. Mine is down in seconds, but Kerry takes one sniff and is feeling sick. I notice she is pale and her lips somewhat blue. I tell her, then to calm her look of horror assure her it's a normal sign of oxygen starvation. Would she like some aspirin? I've been popping one every few hours to thin my blood, since its gets awfully thick and sluggish at heights. She'll need to eat something to take it, I say, so she sips at her soup. The plan works. We each offer her some piece of 'helpful' advice as how to cope best with her malady. She suffers us patiently. Then follows *pomme* mash and roast beef slices with onions – fresh out of the microwave I'm sure but it's hot and I'm gulping. Dan and Paul eat well enough but Kerry pokes and picks with a dizzy head so I'm happy with the left-overs till I can fit no more. Eric has stopped on his salami, feeling headachy too now. A team of Bosnian climbers keeps us entertained: big men, my two metres tall with miles more beef. One, the slightest, looks like a cross between Doug Scott and John

Lennon. We don't know now but they are on a tight budget, their only rope a few yards of 6mm cord which they tie to with a bowline. No harnesses or fancy kit. They've had a war and one hasn't climbed for twenty years. They smoke like troopers – in the hut too for us all to 'enjoy' – but this is France and smoking was the norm inside public spots at that time.

Sleep a little fitful and cold at first. I'm wishing for my sleeping bag but after wrapping myself with eight or so extra blankets I've rustled together I'm warming and drying out. By two a.m. I'm sweltering so layers off and sleep only in thermals. A good sign. Dan sleeps not a wink, Eric and Kerry rise feeling 'poorly', especially Kerry as she's just getting over a flu and with barely anything down her yesterday and a thin little thing to begin with, there isn't much in reserve.

The dawn is clear but blustery. I'm out early and meditating in the sunlight, looking at the ridge before us and there, on its top, the glittering rectangle of the Gouter Hut. It looks closer than I had expected and the 'Bowling Alley', with so much snow, appears unlikely to unleash stones. Some team was up early obviously, for there are tracks across the snowfield to the foot of the couloir. There I can make out the steel cable lifeline spanning its eighty yards or so. It looks safer than they say and I'm confident we'll be up the ridge in an easy four or five hours.

No breakfast for Eric and Kerry though, and not a good sign. Kerry just manages a bowl of tea with two sugar cubes in it, though I finish the dregs ("I've lived in Africa you know"). For me I'm happy with prunes, dates, and muesli bars to save dosh on the hut brekky. We're off by 7.30 a.m., as late as I'd like to be. Eric breaks trail and we follow until we come to what looks like a crevasse. He's already over it so we detour and fall behind. Eric is steaming up the snowfield to the bowling alley. We catch him some one hour later and he's puffed as they come. Behind us follow the three Spaniards (again!), the seven-man Bosnian crew, and one or two smaller ropes. And already there are parties coming up the ridge from the Nid d'Aigle tram line. The first day of sun on the hill and out they come in droves. Better keep on moving.

It's a new fast party of three that passes us to be first on the fixed cable across the bowling alley. Conditions are as good as can be – deep snow means slowed down rock fall if any at all. The first team, methinks a guide with clients, clips into the line and moves across fast enough, one at a time. I'm next and already looking at the steep pitch that follows at the end of it. Here is no place for a fall as there is a bluff below and an icefall below that. It will go better with the rope so when I'm across I'm rigging the belay for Eric to lead when he's ready. He brings up the rear, clips into my belay line and is off in thigh deep fifty-five degree powder on rock. Skating a bit here as we left our crampons off for the deep snow, but now wishing we had them as ice coats the wee rock ledges. Finally Eric has the rope fastened and I've already got the three hitched onto the newly fixed rope with prussiks so they can ascend this section with joy. The mountain strewn with folk below us. Two of the Spaniards have turned back for some reason, their third passes us un-roped and alone. I find out later from him in broken French-Anglo-Spanish that they turned back in fear. Taking one look up the ridge you can hardly blame them. This is a daunting environment and we puny mites in it. The way now narrowed on an ever-steepening snow-covered 1600-foot rock-ridge with terrific exposure all the way to the front door of the Gouter hut. If someone were to slip out of the hut door (and with the ice up there it remains a distinct possibility!), he might bounce a couple of times before hurtling past us on the ridge and sliding into the icefall another five hundred feet below us, probably in several pieces.

With our rope pitch over we untie and head up a steep snow slope to find a ledge where we can stop and put on crampons. Dan waiting patiently and obviously comfortable on this kind of ground. It will be a slow day of leapfrog. Five people on a ridge to protect, but too big a ridge to use the rope the whole way. So we economize and sometimes Eric or I lead with a running belay, covering long pitches up to two hundred feet and placing a sling or piece of protection every now and again. Sometimes we go un-roped. Sometimes there is fixed cable in the really steep sections, and we gladly hold on to these as needed. We are amazed to be passed by guides dragging heaving clients up the hill, strung together by a few feet of old rope. One decent error on the part of either one of the two clients and the guide will be pulled off the mountain and they'll all die. But they seem to know this ridge like the back of their hand and weave their way back and forth, traipsing the rope over every natural rock spike or protrusion in order to gain at least some small amount of protection in the event of a slip.

We stop a few times, at one point sharing a ledge with the Bosnian boys, one of whom delighted us by popping a prune into each of our mouths just as we grunted up the last step to join them. They work by blasting up a couple hundred feet of hill together (in two ropes, one of three and one of four), then stopping for a cigarette and a laugh, before moving off. They are obviously enjoying themselves. All steepens considerably near the top, and we see a helicopter dropping supplies at the ridge overhead. Clouds of spindrift whirl about – the chopper doesn't land as it's too exposed a point. Must be quite a wind up there as every now and again we see a stream of spindrift shear off at hundred yards on the horizontal into the air. It's increasingly windy for us too, and near the top we're tired and hauling on every fixed line we come to. One guide passes us with two dead-beat looking clients, chiding us for our method. Well, yes thanks for the advice mate but we're not letting go. And what are you going to do about it, throw us off? Call the alpine police? We press on un-fazed.

At last we're there. The place is milling with well over sixty people, more as the evening wears on and the stragglers trudge in from above and below. Eric now feeling really 'crook' – that's my word - and hits the pit without food or water. It's bright still – we've been on the go for eight hours. Five o'clock and it will be light until ten at least. I'm parched so we buy six bottles of water and drink on Dan's plastic bill. Some of the guides are rehydrating on beer. The tables are full to bursting with sun burnt, mountain-browned lined faces laughing, talking, joking, silent, staring in a multitude of languages and signs. My back is sore and I am certainly pooped, but well enough I think with the altitude, though glad for the aspirin. Kerry a bit out of it, blue lips again, but she's up and talking so there's a good thing, we say. Dan and Paul are going well - Dan proving an exceptionally strong and competent scrambler and could have done without the ropes or fixed cables I'm sure on the way up, and Paul quietly fit and with loads in reserve, I reckon, physically and psychologically. Food goes well with me – pasta with big chunks of brazed tender meat cooked in wine and mushroom and onion – that after soup and followed by caramel custard. After, I gear up for tomorrow, summit day. The weather is looking superb, and I pack lightly.

Then Eric appears looking like death with an announcement: I'm not going up tomorrow. I'm going down in the morning. Then he disappears back to his pit. Already we had been talking about the dangers of descending the ridge, how we were dreading going back down it, how Eric and I could protect the steeper sections with two ropes and work the belays. It would be slow, it would be painful, it might take all day, but it could be done. Could be. But now Eric wants to go down alone – he'd take one of the two ropes to be sure and possibly abseil the steeper sections. But could he manage? He was ill as they come, weakened from altitude, dehydration and lack of food. But you don't argue with Eric, not when he's like this. He's stubborn as an ox, affirms Dan, and once his mind is made up, proposing alternatives is inviting contempt.

I'm all the time thinking of how best to keep us alive. What about a helicopter, I wonder, not for rescue, but as an alternative descent – a fitting way off a dangerous hill, as a reward for tomorrow's summit efforts, successful or not? I mention it to the others and I think they think I am joking, but eventually I persuade Dan with his French to ask the hut manager if the helicopter company did tourist flights to and from the hut, and if so, how much? Watching his conversation from a distance, it doesn't sound too hopeful at first. The manager is shaking his head - *non, non, non, non monsieur* – but it turns out he thinks we are asking to get a freebie return ride with the supply helicopter. Once he hears we want a *tourist* flight, and are happy to pay, he makes a phone-call for us and gets the details. Yes, the helicopter company does do pickups from certain places in the mountains, including the Gouter Hut. Yes, they could manage a maximum of five people with packs. Yes, they could do it tomorrow, weather permitting, though we'd have to call nearer the time to confirm the arrangement. And the cost? Five thousand francs all told; that equates to five hundred quid split five ways: a hundred quid each. It had to be the answer. We could make for the summit – whoever was up to it that was - return to the hut, then fly out together happy and safe. No splitting up. No death on descent. No risking our necks down that ridge. No more expensive nights in huts – for we'd have to spend at least fifty pounds more again each if we were to go down the ordinary way in hut fees alone, let alone in water! And one of us could catch a bus or train down to Les Houches from the helicopter base in Argentière to get the car. Easy. It was certain.

But Eric would have nothing to do with it. All our persuading and cajoling and offering to pay his seat was to no avail, and seemed only to elicit scorn. Was it the money? The ethics? He wouldn't say. He had sunk into a depressed, morose state from which we were powerless to extricate him. Our elation turned to misery. We were still bent on the helicopter. We just couldn't *not* use it. But what would we say to his wife, if he were to die struggling to climb down ill, while we flew down in splendid safety? The whole helicopter thing, far from being our salvation, looked like being the wedge that would split us in two. We didn't know it then, but Eric later confided that as we were bedding down in the bunk that night, he was awake with the thought that he would probably never see his family again. He knew the ridge was a desperate and dangerous climb alone, especially in his condition. Just before he rolled over to sleep next to me, I turned to him: Eric, you know I really don't like the idea of you going down that ridge alone. That was all I could say. I put in my ear plugs, crossed myself, and began my prayers.

Eric ice bouldering on the glacier above the Col du Grand Montets, France, 2015.

CHAPTER NINETEEN

NO PICNIC ON MONT BLANC: PART III

Two a.m. and it's bedlam again. Forty or more people in this section of the hut are thrashing about, putting on inner boots, outer boots, salopettes, fleeces, jackets, balaclavas, gloves, gaiters, headlights, helmets, packing and repacking stuff sacks, but all in a strange kind of tired, nervous silence. It's summit day. I'm dressed quickly and gather my things and just before leaving the bunk room, I squeeze Eric's foot. He looks up. I say nothing, but raise my hand in silent farewell. He does his and I walk from the room to put on my boots. My insides are tense, but when I brace myself against the cold over the foul-smelling chasm which is one of the toilet holes, I am unsuccessful. Eric is going down and I fear he may die doing it. Kerry wants to go up today – or at least she's giving in to encouragement to do so – but really should be staying here. In fact we should all be staying here, technically speaking. We are not ready for a 16,000 foot hill. Yet I'm feeling confident myself, fit enough. What can stop us now? Today I shall climb Mont Blanc. I'm packed and order a bowl of tea. My dried fruit and pumpernickel don't go down as well as I'd like, and I force the tea down knowing I'll need every drop of fluid. I watch in pain as someone returns his breakfast tray to the kitchen with a full cup of juice, which is summarily poured down the sink. That juice could save someone's life, I think. The others join me, and Kerry I think gets some hot chocolate into her. Dan and Paul eat a few crumbs. We're all tired of muesli bars.

Just then, Eric stomps in. "I'm coming," he says with a grimace. He's not happy. He looks terrible. He won't say why, and we won't ask. But inside I'm so relieved, and, I know, so are the others. Well, we had better get moving. Parties have already started out. It's half two and it's time to go. I put on gaiters and crampons and I'm out on the terraced ice ramp leading up the corniced snow ridge, ready and waiting. But there's a hitch. Kerry has lost her headlight. Everyone looks for it, but it's gone. She can manage without, I say. It's a bright night, and on Eric's suggestion I offer to rope her to me for added security. Still I wait. I'm getting cold. Shall I put on my bigger mitts? I don't want to, since I know I'll start heating up once we get going. But my feet are getting cold. Numb even. I stamp them. I swing my arms. Eric comes out at last, but then I see he hasn't even got his gaiters on. I watch him go about putting them on, laboriously, fiddling with apparently insignificant things, like whether to lie down or stand up his ice axe next to him while he crampons up. After trying several times to stick his ice-axe upright in the snow, he finds the ground too frozen and hard, so he lies it down, but then it threatens to skitter away, off the edge, so he leans it against his pack, but then as he lets go it falls down, so he tries it head side down. Still no good. Finally he strikes the pick of his axe into the frozen snow. It sticks. Now he can get back to his gaiter. Oops, wrong foot. Have to undo the salopettes zip again to get the gaiter on under it, with the salopettes leg over the top. Loop of the gaiter won't fit over the boots. I moan inwardly. Is he going to have to take off his boots? No. He struggles and yanks it, then it comes. He can't do the zip up with his mitts on. He takes them off. Then he takes off his gloves, leaving his inner gloves. He does the zip. He fastens the velcro. He hooks the stud into his front lace. Too tight? Try the next lace back. Hmm. Too loose. Better back to the front lace. Now zip back the salopettes leg. Do up the velcro. Oops. Dropped a glove. I pick it up speedily. 'Can I help with anything?' I bark impatiently. No. Now he starts on his other foot. I crunch off to see how the others are getting on. They don't have their crampons on yet either. And so it goes on.

Finally, we are the last group to leave but one: a middle-aged Canadian mountaineering couple are right behind us. Not long after they turn back in the wind, she ill with altitude. The snow conditions are perfect. Sixty or more pairs of cramponed boots have trumped the soft snow down into a nice firm little track, and I lead and settle into a steady, slow rhythm, rope trailing behind me to Kerry. Looking up into the darkness we see a long line of lights, like a vast string of pilgrims setting out up some sacred mountain. We are gaining slowly, but there's no effort to. Just a slow, steady pace I say. An hour or two pass, and Dan takes over in front. The wind has increased, and the tracks are filling up with snow. Great drifts move across the hill like sand. The sky lightens almost imperceptibly in the east. Our route having left the ridge of the Aiguille du Gouter ascends the long featureless western slopes of the Dome du Gouter. At its top we breast the broad col to a fierce, icy blast, the eastern sky cold and bluing, the sharp skyline now visible as a jagged and endless sweep of icy mountains and ridges. Away to the east there sits the tall cold Aiguille du Midi, beyond it still the huge Aiguille Verte and the dark rock towers of the Dru. Is that the Matterhorn way beyond in Switzerland? And the Grand Combin? Or is it Monta Rosa in Italy? It is difficult to look up with the wind-driven spindrift lashing my face like icy daggers. My goggles are still in my pack, so I pull my hood down and press on down the other side of the col. From here now we can see the summit ridge, though the summit itself is hiding just out of sight. Clouds of spindrift are blasting horizontally off the top hundreds of metres into Italy. Finally the sun rises and we stop to goggle up. A slurp of cold water and more stamping of the boots. My left foot and right hand are quite numb. It's sure cold, I say. Do I take a photo? I don't remember. The rope comes off Kerry and I coil it in my pack. No place to stop for long in this wind so we press on down the slope from which we eventually take the diagonal line up towards the Vallot refuge hut at 4360 metres, shimmering in the dawn sun. Only metres from it we see someone on skis, lying down on the slope, motionless. On arrival we see why. The slope is bare hard ice – no death run out, but a nasty tumble and slide and impossible to cut along with skis. He can't move up or down, and is worn out with trying to get them off. But he'll survive. My crampons bite but the ice axe is useless. Kerry and Paul thrash and struggle, feeling the precariousness in the new experience of teetering on rock-hard ice. Dan sticks with them so Eric and I make it to the hut, perched on a rocky outcrop exposed to the full force of the bitter easterly wind.

It is a sorry sight inside. The Vallot suffers serious neglect and is little more than a rubbish tip. But it has saved some lives and inside we are out of the wind at least. There are four German climbers supine, dozing fitfully on the floor wrapped in blankets but looking cold. Four Bosnians look at us arriving, the lustre and sparkle gone from their faces. A Spanish crew are messing about with their ropes, treading on them, rubbish and plastic skewered and stuck to their crampons. There too is one of the French guides with her two clients, looking worn-out and ready to descend. Eric tugs his duvet weakly from his pack. I help him into it, then he drops in a heap in the corner, arms folded, knees up, eyes closed, mouth agape, head lolled sideways. I add my fleece and big mitts, stamping my feet and swinging my arms, getting some circulation back in painful, throbbing stabs. The others arrive at last, and I help them through the trapdoor entry hole. Kerry too flops down on the perished mattress next to Eric. Paul covers her with his jacket, then scrounges up another dirty old blanket from the corner for her. You can cover her with all you like, I say coldly, but it won't do her any good if she's not producing any heat. We three stand there studying them like specimens, until Dan I think has the sense to sit between them in an attempt to offer them his warmth. There are no hot drinks here. It's way sub-zero inside, and we chat a bit, managing a laugh and a quip just to show that we are still in control. Kerry retches into her glove, Paul encourages her to use the floor. In minutes it will be frozen forever. It's an ingenious way to leave your mark on the world. I drink more and eat a date. One date. It's all I can manage, though I recall longing for an apple.

Only 450 metres above lies the summit, perhaps an hour and a half at a steady pace. But looking out the window of the Vallot, I can see the final Bosses ridge is out of the question. I say as much. Eric hears and agrees. With a pair of experienced climbers in acclimatized condition, the ridge in this kind of wind would be a serious, though achievable undertaking. But with Eric out of it, I would prefer not to go it alone, still less to take responsibility for another more dependent partner or three. While the snow conditions were good, the wind was quite capable of throwing you down. And we had all come up here too quickly, and now even the three healthier among us were incapable of stomaching what food we had.

Meanwhile Kerry was turning blue, and she and Eric began shivering uncontrollably. As I watched them I began to chatter myself. We aren't warming up here. We should start going down now. So my pack goes on, but then I see the others have taken their crampons off. It takes an age, Paul on his knees strapping Kerry's to her heavy boots, but finally they are ready to go. No mistakes now, the descent is as demanding as the climb. Nowhere except at the hut entrance are we exposed to a death fall like the day before, but the wind is as strong as ever and the cold can kill as quickly as anything else. I am slow. Many stops with deep breathing is the only way to go. Even on Huascaran at 22,000 feet I don't remember being this heavily affected. Eric takes the front on the way back up the dome, but later I pass him slumped in the snow. He's okay he says, so I press on now and don't turn back. All the way I go. Down and down. There are no tracks, just deep drifts through which I plunge endlessly. Did we really come up all this way? Now I can enjoy the view. Bionassay rears up beautifully, an icy, cornice-ridged beauty inviting an ascent for another day, another life. Minutes pass into hours and still I go on. At the very bottom of the dome I turn at last and spy the hill behind. There is Eric, moving still. That's good. Higher up, there are the other three, Dan and Paul sticking with Kerry. She'll be okay. Other parties too are zig-zagging down the slope. I turn and continue. Just near the hut at last, I stop and wait. There is a steep step here, awkward and exposed. It wouldn't be right to slip to one's death twenty yards from safety. So I rig a belay and wait in the sun and wind and spindrift, dreaming and warming. Finally they come, worn out, silent but cheery. Dan goes ahead. He'll be seeing about the helicopter tonight. I ask the time and it's only 10.30 a.m.

But when I reach the hut, bringing up the rear, Paul has a happy message. Helicopter's on the way. It'll be here in half an hour. I whoop with elation. Just time to gather the kit. I'll take that rope Eric. Anything else, anyone? I jam it all into my pack, now twice it's normal weight, and thrash on up the deep snow to the landing zone on the ridge just behind the hut. What a puff! These last thirty yards seem as hard as the previous thousand! Just time to rig a safety line for the others again. No slips here please. Then we are joined by one of the guides from the hut who is out to check the wind speed. It's calmer here than up the hill: "Fifty to sixty kilometres, east, south-east," he shouts into his radio. I gasp – is it too fast? "Pas problem!" he announces loudly with a smile.

We wait with cocked heads, listening for the 'wop' of the blades. We see it first, a tiny speck of a shadow grinding its way up the glacier below. Then the sounds come reflecting off the mountain to us, and before long it roars in from behind us, over the fatal drop, and as it rests lightly on the snow with props at full chop, spindrift blasts us flat. At the signal I'm away, propelled through deep snow by sheer adrenaline, towing the others in my wake. Belts on, gloves off, camera out, packs in, then suddenly the door is closed, the rotors scream and we're away – a wave to our hut guide as the blades take the load and we swoop down over the snow shelf like a speeding bird. Eric's reaching for something to grab hold of but it's just lean and go with the flow on one of these machines, trusting pilot and g-force to do their bit. As we settle into a steadier descent, the alps open out before us, vast sweeping rock and ice faces, supernal vistas of crevasse and serac and icefall. There's the whole of the Grand Mulet and Bosses glaciers, winding their way up to Mont Blanc's shining summit. There's the Midi, so elegant from this angle, with the ever so delicate arete of the Frendo Spur dropping clean away from its tops. There are the countless rocky Chamonix Aiguilles, and the long, winding dragon's tail of the Mer de Glace, which in years to come I would descend solo on skis, and further south still the huge north face of the Grandes Jorasses looking austere and impressive as ever. Then comes the Dru, dark and sinister and ice-laced as if wintered still, so early are we in the season. Pine trees fly past now as we pass from white to green, dropping all the while with Chamonix stretched out below us like a lazy, sleeping cat. Over the telepherique line for the Grand Montets, then suddenly a dive clean off the edge down into the Argentière glacial gorge. Eric's panicking and starting to swoon, but the dive only steepens as we cut left and blast down between the towering cliff sides at right angles, massive seracs only feet below. Then it's another impossible cut right, improbably fast, crushed to our seats and all squealing with terror-filled delight. Then there's the base, a tiny square way lower yet but in seconds a broad acre of asphalt, and we're down on *terra firma*, rotors slowing and we sweltering in the sudden heat. Bravo! shouts Dan, and it's *merci buckets* all round except for Eric who retires to the shade, fighting back the nausea and the sheer, shocking incredulity of it all.

So what more can I say? It was the whimps' way out, that's for sure. Eight minutes to cover what might have killed us over two days – a hundred pounds poorer but at the time I had no quibbles about the rightness of it all. I would see my wife and son again. So would Eric his! Just a shame to leave all those suffering bods at the Gouter with a fight still before them and most without the easier option. Two hours' later we were sat at table minus Eric with beer and salad on the way. Kerry had revived almost instantly, but it was to be another gut-wrenching twenty-four hours for Eric before he could take even a cup of tea, let alone a meal. As far as he was concerned, that was the end of his high-altitude climbing career. How would he ever live it down with his nine year-old son who so desperately wants to climb K2? As it turned out, all of us along with Eric were forced to settle in our own way with the fact that what had started out as a serious climbing trip would amount in mountaineering terms to little more than a pleasurable tourist jaunt. A picnic after all! For Dan, Paul, and Kerry, there was no shame in that. For me, consolation lay in the fact that I would live - again - to tell the story. For Eric, perhaps the most morally conscientious climber of us all, the simultaneous relief and disappointment was to become the catalyst for no small degree of intestinal and emotional havoc in the days that followed.

Since that first escapade in the French Alps, I have been back four more times, in both winter and summer seasons: hiking in the forests and alpine hills, climbing waterfall ice in the Argentière valley, skiing solo and off piste in the Valle Blanche, mixing rock and ice in the Aiguille de Tour range and on the Aiguille du Midi. I still haven't succeeded on my lifelong dream climbs: the great north face routes on Les Courtes and Les Vertes, and of course the elusive Mont Blanc, yet another mountain I have never climbed. Each year Eric sends me an open invitation to meet up with him and his now well-accomplished alpinist son. I guess I will just have to keep on trying, keep on remembering, keep on dreaming.

Plan de l'Aiguille, Chamonix, France, 2015.

Above the Grand Montets col, Glacier d' Argentiere behind.
French Alps, 2015

CHAPTER TWENTY
BURGLAR IN LANGTANG

They say that once you start climbing in the Himalayas your chances of dying in the mountains soar exponentially. I didn't want to die but I had always wanted to climb the tallest mountains on earth. After Peru my Irish friend Tony and I outlined plans to climb Ama Dablam near Everest, and I even corresponded with Michael Kennedy, somewhat presumptuously in retrospect, to get route information from his remarkable 1985 winter ascent of the northeast face with Carlos Buhler. Within four months of returning from the Diamond Couloir in 1990, however, I got married and all future plans to climb in the Himalaya, or anywhere serious for that matter, were put on ice. In fact already before Mt Kenya my life had been changing direction. I didn't strap on crampons again for almost a decade.

I never regretted this shift in vocational focus. For a while I had contemplated a professional career in climbing, and I don't think this would have been unrealistic, despite my mediocre abilities and accomplishments. But I had begun to wonder what my climbing was doing to serve anyone beyond myself, and felt myself increasingly drawn towards a religious vocation where my intellectual gifts could be deployed in higher educational research and for the hopeful betterment of others.

Although my new life did not afford me the luxury of flying off for regular climbing expeditions several months a year, as I had been used to, my love for the mountains never waned, and an opportunity to climb at last in the Himalaya presented itself on our return to Australia in 2002 after three years away studying in the UK. My wife Lizzy had long dreamed of trekking in Nepal, and our son Ben was now ten years old, a seasoned walker, and open to a high altitude walking adventure. I wrote to the Nepal Mountaineering Association requesting permission to climb one of the lower trekking peaks in the Langtang Himal, Naya Kanga. At 5844m (19,100 ft), Naya Kanga, otherwise known as Gunja la Chuli, costs less than the "Category A" trekking peaks in Nepal. Its northeast ridge presents a modest but attractive-enough and viable mountaineering target at the head of the Langtang Valley. It's not that high or difficult by anyone's climbing standards, but this was going to be a family tour, and I didn't want to tackle anything too risky or demanding. By organizing our own expedition, the total cost of the trip, including peak fee, two climbing Sherpas, along with the requisite cook, kitchen crew, porters, transport from

Kathmandu, and insurance, ended up coming to under US$3000.

The year 2002 turned out to be both a bad year and a good year to visit Nepal. The bad side of it was that the Nepalese Civil War between the Maoist Communist Party and Government forces re-erupted that year with peculiar vehemence. In June 2001 virtually the entire Nepalese Royal Family were massacred in one hit. Urgent peace talks were organized in an effort to stem further bloodshed and retaliation. On our arrival in April 2002, diplomatic efforts had broken down and the social tension and fear were palpable, with many police, military and security personnel exploiting the political situation as a licence for unrestrained cruelty and violence. In May, right when we were completing our trek, the peace talks failed, and widespread strikes, insurgency, and lawlessness broke out afresh, escalating in the months that followed. The result was that during 2002 more people died from the war than in any other year of its ten-year duration (some 17,000 overall).

The good side was that, due to most foreigners cancelling their travel arrangements, we had the Langtang Valley almost completely to ourselves. Our small caravan of porters, kitchen staff, sherpas and ourselves snaked its way from the cool monkey-inhabited forests of the lower valley up between the towering faces of the big 7000-plus metre Langtang Lirung and Langtang Ri peaks unaffected by pathway or camp-site congestion. Our son Ben proved to be a curiosity to the local village people, especially the children. Perhaps they didn't often see western children trekking in these mountains. They would often swarm around him, taking his hand in theirs, stroking his honey-blond hair, laughing, staring, and apparently enchanted by this mysterious pint-sized human phenomenon. At first Ben was bit overwhelmed by the attention, particularly when he first experienced it in the bustling and busy streets of Kathmandu. But here in the broad open spaces of the mountains he seemed to feel safer, and during one of our unscheduled rest days - precipitated by a nasty bout of gastro - Ben spent the whole day playing with a lass who had sidled up alongside him chattering in Nepali. Despite the language barrier they mucked around like old time friends.

The trek from the road-end at Syabrubesi (1,460m) to Kyanjin Ghompa (3,800m) near the end of the Langtang Kola took a leisurely five days, including rest days. At Langtang Village our tents were just about destroyed by a freak thunderstorm that struck with fury. At one point in the night, as the storm was reaching its wild pitch, Ben, who was sleeping between me and Lizzy, sat bolt upright and declared fretfully that he wanted to go home. It took several night-time visits from our two Sherpas, who were up all night keeping the tents secure and who regularly checked on our wellbeing, for Ben to gain enough reassurance finally to lie down again before night's end.

Of course Langtang Village is no more. It was destroyed by a landslide in April 2015 after the massive earthquake that struck the region and caused death on Everest. Over three hundred people were killed in the Langtang landslide, and more than a hundred bodies, including those of numerous foreign trekkers, still lie buried beneath the debris, never to be recovered.

Our arrival in Kyanjin Ghompa coincided with two events: news of the outbreak of strikes and insurgency after failed peace talks in the capital, and the early onset of the monsoon season. Heavy flakes of snow fell as the porters pitched our tents on the northern fringe of the village. Only the shoulder of Kyanjin Ri (4773m), immediately behind and northeast of the village, was visible. Our own target, Naya Kanga, was swathed in a thick blanket of low cloud. A sense of inevitable finality settled upon us, as we spent the next day drinking tea in the tent or in one of the local chai houses, gloomily watching the snow fall. Our sherpas Dendi and Pasang interpreted the snow as a sure sign of the monsoon, with its threat of more snow and increased avalanche risk. Pasang especially also talked up the political crisis: it would be better for us, he urged, to get back to Kathmandu as soon as possible, before strikes and curfews made getting to the airport and leaving the country impossible. It seemed obvious that they were happy to call it quits. They spent the day crammed in the warm cook tent, playing cards and buffooning around with the kitchen staff and remaining porters.

That evening, we agreed to pack up early and head home. We still had five days planned here at Kyanjin Ghompa, enough time to climb the peak had the weather been friendly. We were not scheduled to be back in Kathmandu for another eight days or so, and there was no guarantee we could arrange an earlier flight out to Bangkok and then on to Adelaide via Sydney. Ben had coped exceptionally well with the altitude, with no noticeable ill effects, and it seemed a shame to abandon the expedition after all had gone so well. As we wriggled into our sleeping bags, with snow still falling outside the tent, I became aware of the old dismal feeling of yet another failed expedition. It was as if I was doomed never to succeed as a mountaineer. Once again there would be no epic ascent through treacherous conditions. No triumphant elation on summit day. No heroic return to basecamp. No remarkable story to tell. I lay there, listening to the patter of snow and the steady breathing of my wife and son, and wondered how I might redeem the situation and accomplish something worthy of the universal mountaineering spirit. Perhaps in the morning, while the others started down the valley, I could race up to the summit of Kyanjin Ri, if only to release some of the pent-up energy and hope that churned around unfulfilled and unrealized inside me. If I moved fast and all went well, I could easily catch them up by sundown, perhaps even by lunchtime. Maybe Dendi would agree to accompany me? From my conversations with him he seemed the more adventurous of the two sherpas, driven less by entrepreneurship and careerism and more by sheer love of climbing.

As I lay there dreaming my plans, dozing in the half-world between wakefulness and sleep, I vaguely heard the zip on our tent slide open. Lizzy must be going out for some reason, I thought. With my right hand I sleepily reached for my headlight, which I kept by my head, and with my left reached over towards her, expecting to find an empty space, but instead I found that she was still lying there curled on her side, fast asleep. I sprang into wakefulness, suddenly conscious that the zip had been opened from the outside, and that there was someone rummaging around through our stuff in the vestibule. Twisting on my headlight and unzipping the inner tent, I called out "Hey! Who's there?" and launched myself through the open flap into the vestibule. I saw a dark body reel back and run towards a nearby stone wall, launch over it, and disappear with a terrific crash and splash on the other side. As I clumsily pulled my boots on, I called for help: "Pasang! Dendi! Come, come! Thief! Thief! Pasang! Dendi!" By now Lizzy and Ben had woken and were fearfully asking what was wrong, and I could hear Pasang and Dendi's voices from their tent. With my boots just on I stumbled after the intruder, following his tracks through the snow towards the stone wall. By the time I reached it, standing there in my long-johns and boots, Pasang and Dendi had caught up, and we shone our headlight beams over the wall. It was a wide but shallow sewage pit. The corrugated iron that loosely covered it had collapsed with the intruder's weight, and he had plunged headlong into the watery shit below. Somehow before we got to him he had managed to scramble out and make his escape, but had left a dirty stinking trail in the fresh snow which eventually disappeared in the messed up muddy lanes between the houses back towards the centre of the village.

What he had been after is anyone's guess. Boots, most likely. But he didn't find any. Even in these snowy conditions, we kept our boots and most of our gear inside the tent proper, along with our money and passports. Outside in the vestibule we had left only a stuff sac or two of some food and an empty pack. I wondered whether he had been tipped off that this was our last night. We would never know. I half-thought of launching an investigation the next day, as it wouldn't be hard to sniff the culprit out; but on our trek in we had seen how violently rural Nepalese treated alleged petty thieves among their own, viciously beating and publicly humiliating the accused in question, and I figured this fellow's run-in with the septic pool had served punishment enough.

In the morning I floated my plan to race up Kyanjin Ri with Dendi, who welcomed the proposal with enthusiasm, and so after breakfast, as Lizzy and Ben headed down valley with the rest of the team, Dendi and

I turned uphill and made for a quick ascent of the peak. Despite the fresh snow, the terrain was easy and the cloud layer lifted, granting us splendid views of the village below, though Naya Kanga, situated immediately opposite us across the valley, remained hidden from view.

We paused on the summit only briefly, for a drink and a breather, before tearing off back down the mountain, whooping and bounding like children. Once back in the valley, we trotted and galloped along the path in our big alpine boots, alive with the thrill of even a minor accomplishment and the vigor and grace of good health. Sure enough, we caught up with the others by lunch-time just past the village of Mundu (3550m). The trek back down to Syabrubesi felt entirely different from the way up; it rained most nights and our porters, some shod only in rubber thongs, slipped often, one spraining his ankle just below Lama Hotel. His colleagues rendered first aid by holding him down and lashing the affected ankle with huge stinging nettles, while he squirmed and hollered in pain. Within half an hour he was up and toting his load again down the slippery trail.

The five-hour bus journey to Kathmandu via Dhunche and Trisuli Bazaar passed with no more than the usual discomforts induced by suffocating diesel smoke, dust, heat, sweat, and minor break-downs, though there were now more check points along the road, and Kathmandu seemed noticeably more chaotic. Sorting gear and resting up at our Blue Diamond Hotel, we succeeded in re-arranging earlier flights all the way through to Adelaide; though on the day we were due to leave strikes had come into force, security had been stepped up, and flights were delayed. The road to the airport was clogged with traffic; the airport had been cordoned off and only ticket-holders were being admitted beyond the checkpoint. We were forced to disembark a good half-kilometre away from the terminal and lug our four giant duffle bags of kit between the three of us. It was a relief to flop down at our departure gate to sit out the delay.

When at last we were called to board, we saw that our luggage had actually not yet been loaded, but was laid out in a long line on the tarmac. Along with the two hundred or so other passengers, we were herded outside into a group in front of the jet, then told to walk over and select our own items of luggage from the line and load them into the giant luggage containers ourselves. Guessing that the odd process was intended as a precaution to prevent a bomb being sneaked on board, we soon found out why. When finally all the luggage had been accounted for and all passengers seated and the doors ready to close, a fancily dressed dignitary accompanied by two visibly armed bodyguards boarded and sat down in the front row. It was Nepal's Prime Minister Sher Bahadur Deuba. It seems we had been allotted the most secure flight out of Kathmandu that day. I have never been able to discover why he was headed to Bangkok at that moment, but it could have been related to the fact that he was in the throes of being expelled from his own party in the increasingly turbulent political crisis. Nepal was falling apart, and he was preparing for the worst.

With this modest foray in the Himalaya completed, and counting the ascent of Kyanjin Ri a little improperly as a "climb", I realized during the long flights home that I had now climbed mountains on six of the earth's seven continents. At first it sounded like a spectacular achievement, and I was tempted to entertain a self-aggrandizing view of myself, until I admitted that most of my climbs had been a flop, and that the few successful ventures amounted in any case to pretty average climbing accomplishments, comparatively speaking. I would have to accept my limits, and acknowledge my status as a mountaineering mediocrity, an average and ordinary man, whose romantic aspirations seemed destined never to be realizable in the flesh. Yet through it all I knew myself to be remarkably blessed by these experiences, and even if I had not exploited to the full all the extraordinary opportunities that had come my way, I had nevertheless been dramatically and permanently changed by them, and by the diverse, unique, and beloved people with whom I had shared them. I trusted it was all for the better.

Copeland Shelter, New Zealand, 1987.

CHAPTER TWENTY-ONE
THE NEED FOR SPEED

Speed climbing is all the rage today. On the internet you regularly come across news of some well-known route being completed in a new record time. The Nose of El Cap or the Nordwand of the Eiger in under three hours. Mont Blanc or the Matterhorn in under four hours - return! Everest base camp to summit in eight hours. Almost invariably the records are solo achievements, for that is by far and away the fastest, lightest, most efficient way to climb a route, unencumbered by all the equipment, clutter, and negotiation necessitated by a partnered or belayed climb. Why climb fast? Is it just to break records? Speed is safety, as all mountaineers know. But go too fast and you risk errors in judgement. Why climb solo? Isn't it foolhardy? Summing up the experience of so many others, Steve House, one of the most accomplished alpinists ever, says he always found profoundest meaning and greatest reward in climbing fast and alone. "My most rewarding days were days when I cut away everything; when I redefined my understanding of necessity."[10]

While I am no sport climber or super-alpinist, and have never nor will ever set anything close to a record in the mountains, I have often found myself racing solo up a climb towards a summit against the clock, and I dare say tasting something of the same liberty and clarity of the great solo speed climbers. Sometimes the need for speed has been simply due to bad scheduling. Mostly it has been due to family or work commitments, forcing me to squeeze a climb into a tiny window of limited opportunity. I have already recounted the story of racing up Kyanjin Ri on the morning of our trek out from the head of the Langtang Valley. Like many of my snatched ventures it was a more or less vain or valiant attempt to redeem a failed plan. It seems to follow a pattern that has appeared with frequency through my adult life.

Take for example my winter solo of Great End in Borrowdale. It had started out as a leisurely family drive on a cold winter's day in Northumbria. We decided to cross the Pennines from Durham and head for the Cumbrian Lake District. After lunch in Keswick, we headed along the road to Borrowdale, parking at Seathwaite Farm at the road end. There my travel companions seemed to want to do little more than potter

---

[10] Steve House, *Beyond the Mountain* (Sheffield: Vertebrate Publishing, 2010), xi.

around and maybe explore the track up by the long stepped waterfall, where once I had seen an unwary climber, plodding across a frozen pond to his next pitch, break through the ice-crust and plunge backwards into the deep pool, submersing his entire body, pack, and helmet in the icy depths. I on the other hand was itching to check out the ice in Central Gully on Great End, about which I had read in Ken Wilson's *Cold Climbs* (1983). I remembered that this classic route was about grade 3 and almost a full day's undertaking, but I figured if I hightailed it I might just have enough time to race up it and be back to the car before I was missed. I wouldn't be long, I said. Only a couple of hours.

    I set off up the frozen path at double pace, my big plastic boots thundering awkwardly beneath me. Nearing the base of the bulking crag I was grateful to find that someone had left a well-formed trail through the soft snow, and I ploughed upwards towards the iced-up gully. In short time I had steamed up the gully to the crux pitch, where I found two parties of climbers queued in turn behind a third party whose leader was on belay and hacking away at the thick blue ice. I looked at my watch to see that I had been gone almost two hours. If I politely waited my turn to solo up the easy bulge of ice, I estimated it would take a further two hours to exit the climb and return to Seathwaite. Alternatively I could ask the leading climber to step aside and let me push on past, but then I figured that wouldn't be cricket, and I would still be pressed for time. So calling it quits, I downclimbed a pitch or two before turning and bashing down the deep snowy gully back towards the valley, clunkily galloping the last kilometre or so down the hard path alongside the Derwent River. When I got back to the car, sweaty and breathless, I had been gone three hours, longer than I had anticipated, but thankfully not long enough to arouse any distemper in my wife and son. Sorry I had not topped out, I nevertheless felt satisfied with the experience and the confidence to which it gave rise, having proved to myself that I was still fit and able to move quickly in steepish winter terrain. Plus I was now able to add Central Gully of Great End to my long list of attempted albeit unclimbed routes.

I seized hold of another snatched opportunity a year or two later in Switzerland beneath the Eiger. Again, the occasion was a family holiday, and I had arranged for us to visit Grindelwald, though given our limited budget had scheduled just two nights there in the cheapest hostel I could find after which we would move on by train through the Alps to Chamonix. It was late winter, and the place was crawling with skiers. The weather on our one free day was mostly fair with high to mid-level cloud, and we joined the hoardes on the cog-train up to the Kleine Scheidegg (2070m), passing beneath the soaring two kilometre-high spectre of the Eiger's north face. Gazing upon its sweeping ice-fields, broken ice-runnels and daunting buttresses, my stomach churned inside with both wonder and dread, as I recalled all that I'd read and studied about this iconic, archetypal nemesis, at the same time aware that none of it did it true justice, nor could prepare anyone for this kind of face-to-face, carnal encounter. I suddenly wanted so much to be on it, to feel for myself its primal power, and wondered how I might get nearer and higher.

Disgorging from the train at Kleine Scheidegg, I felt so awkward and out of place among the pushing and bustling tourists. Proudly I wanted to shout out: "I'm not a tourist. I'm a climber. I don't belong down here. I am supposed to be up there, up that face, on those ridges, hidden, unseen, struggling for my life alongside the mighty, cut off from the nauseating opulence and luxury of cafes and chalets and *apres ski* society." But then my son tugs on my sleeve and asks for a toilet and I am brought back to reality. There's no escaping it: I am one of the barbarian hullabaloo, after all. The ice-axe and crampons strapped to my pack seem suddenly conspicuous, an embarrassing sign of my naïve and fantastical insanity, and I become self-conscious and impatient and angry: with my family, with the endless queues, with the expensively dressed throng, and above all with myself and the inescapable mediocrity of my life.

But casting my eye around, I spy a redemptive opportunity in the form of the Tschuggen, a striking pyramidal peak along the Lauberhorn ridge from the Kleine Scheidegg. In the climbing guidebooks, Tschuggen

(2520m) rates a mention as a summer scramble, and on its western and north-western aspects it is actually surprisingly steep, undercut in places by sheer cliffs and overhanging bluffs. In its winter cloak of snow, it suddenly appeared as an attractive goal, far from the crowds, a point from which I could look back across towards the Eiger's north face at a point about level with the start of the difficulties at the top of the First Pillar. Climbing the Tschuggen would not challenge me technically, but it would get me further into this legendary alpine range, and in some small way promised to satisfy my yearning to get nearer to the Eiger, positioned to scrutinize and perhaps even sense all those features which I felt I knew so well.

With Lizzy and Ben content to explore the snowy plateau around the Jungfraubahn, I plodded off along the snowy track towards Mannlichen. The path traverses around to the upper Honegg ski-lift station situated at the south-eastern base of the Tschuggen. Turning uphill, I was able to ascend the first few hundred feet in narrow diagonals, but as it steepened and the snow hardened, I tackled the angle more directly, keeping close to the right-hand ridge. I can't recall if I donned my crampons or not, but I certainly remember using my axe, nervously aware of the precipitous slide down the south-east face and the yawning exposure off the northern edge of the arete. Arriving at the summit, the view answered to my expectations, and as I sat just below it munching cheese and salami at a safe distance from the sharp drop, I soaked in the visual panorama of the Nordwand with the increased appreciation of having earned it with at least a small degree of mountaineering effort and skill. There was additional satisfaction in the fact that I had come here alone, for there is something both pure and purifying about climbing solo, and wilderness solitude - doubtlessly diminished but not entirely eradicated in busier ranges like this - has its own clarifying power. Below me the busy crowds and chairlifts still buzzed, but here was no sign of anyone: no tracks, no axe or pole holes, no litter. Little did I know that at that moment I was in fact not as alone as I felt, for Lizzy and Ben had patiently watched the final part of my ascent through the telescope, thereby sharing with me, in their own way, my modest and momentary sanctuary from the hubbub.

On at least three other occasions I have made climbs in circumstances similar to these. One was on the Petite Aiguille Verte above Argentière, where I wimped off the summit ridge and spent the three hours before the last lift soloing around on steep glacial features above the Col des Grands Montets. Another was on Victoria's Mt Feathertop where, having raced up through the forest from Harrietville, I found myself - shod in leather hiking boots and without an ice-axe - having to kick seemingly endless steps up the icy, exposed, and heavily corniced summit ridge to the top. Needless to say the descent was precarious. A third, a summer trip this time, was on

Cradle Mountain in Tasmania where, having left Mole Creek at seven a.m., I and a friend set ourselves the rather ambitious goal of driving to Dove Lake, ascending to Cradle Mountain's misty summit, and returning back to Launceston in time to catch a five p.m. flight to Melbourne. It all came together, though I was lucky to avoid getting pinged for speeding on the return drive.

But there is one final speed climb I would like to share, this time made with climbing partner Paul Horne, on the elegant conical volcano that is Mt Taranaki (previously called Mt Egmont) on the north island of New Zealand. In was October 1988, and we had met up in Mt Cook village ten days earlier with the hope of climbing the South Face of Mt Douglas in winter conditions. But the low cloud and rain that had locked the mountains in soggy gloom for the last week or two failed to lift, and we felt increasingly agitated as we helplessly watched any opportunity to climb slipping away.

With only three days before we were due to fly out of Christchurch back to Australia, we cooked up a plan to travel to the north island where, according to the forecasts, the weather was fair, and climb Mt Egmont. By no means was it comparable to the south face of Douglas, either in difficulty or seriousness, but besides being aesthetically pleasing it was something to climb, and right now anything was better than nothing. We managed to book cheap air tickets out of Mt Cook directly to Wellington for the next day, and swap our departing flights back to Melbourne to fly out of Wellington instead. As we took off over the socked in southern alps towards sunnier northern skies, our spirits rose, sensing that we might just pull it off.

Taranaki (2518m) is bigger than it looks on the postcards. We had settled on what looked like the speediest way up via Tahurangi Lodge on the north-east side of the mountain. The drive to New Plymouth from Wellington takes over four hours, so by the time we had our rental car parked by the North Egmont Visitor Centre and had hiked the steep five kilometre track up to Tahurangi Lodge it was late afternoon, too late to ascend and return in softening snow. It was Friday, and our flight out of Wellington was booked for Saturday evening. We would have no time to lose if we were to be back to the car by midday to make the drive.

Around 4 a.m., as we speedily cramponed up the icy north ridge by the light of our headlamps, we felt certain of success. Conditions were perfect: clear, cold, and still. The sun breached the horizon out to our left just before we topped out on the ridge under the brilliant Shark's Tooth. We crossed the crater towards the now brightly sunlit summit cone. A chilly breeze sprang up while we paused for summit photos, and much as we would have liked to ice-boulder on the steep crags encircling the crater we knew we had to scurry to make it down in time. Already the surface ice had softened over a rock-hard icy layer several inches beneath, just out of crampon point range, and the descent proved surprisingly treacherous. My rigid crampons balled up with great wads of wet sticky snow and I utterly trashed my axe-shaft clearing them at every step. Eventually we removed crampons and glissaded in long semi-diagonal tacks, quickly descending what might otherwise have taken considerably longer.

We stopped only to pick up our remaining gear from the hut and refill our water bottles. Like many of my other speed climbs, the final thumping gallop below the snow line down the hard rocky track left me with aching knees and back. I wonder whether my recently developed chronic spinal disintegration is one of the long-term effects of such physical abuse. But of course, as always, despite anxious moments in traffic and queues, we made our flight deadline, and as our aircraft pulled its nose steeply against a stiff Wellington head-wind we finally breathed a sigh of welcome relief, my mind busy with images of what could have gone wrong, but didn't. This time, at least. All was well. Really well. "Thankyou," I breathed. Thankyou. Thankyou.

Adam on the summit of Aiguille Rouge, New Zealand (1987).

Paul Horne on the summit of Mt Sefton, New Zealand (1987).

Paul nearing the summit of Taranaki (Mt Egmont), New Zealand (1988).

CHAPTER TWENTY-TWO
BLOWN OFF MT BULLER

I have always said that the strongest wind I have ever experienced was climbing around Mt Cook in New Zealand. Paul Horne and I had been based at Mueller Hut opposite Mt Sefton's mighty east face, and one night a storm raged to such a fury that we got out of our sleeping bags, packed our rucsacs, and sat fully dressed, boots on, nervously silent while we anxiously contemplated whether to escape the shaking, shuddering hut or be blown away inside it off the ridge.

Not a few New Zealand mountain huts have been blown away in similar circumstances, despite the steel cables anchoring them to the rocky ground. The most infamous accident occurred in 1977 when the Three Johns Hut, situated not far from Mueller Hut on the Barren Saddle, was ripped off its perch with four young climbers inside and blown into the valley below. None survived. Accounts of New Zealand storms speak of a legendary wind 'that seems to harbour intentional fury, even malice.'[11] It is truly a frightening experience to hear a gust of New Zealand mountain wind screaming towards you, building in power, roaring and howling like a set of jet engines at full bore before it slams like a huge wall into your hut, crushing your eardrums and pounding the air out of your lungs, and then doesn't stop, but builds and shakes and batters the entire edifice in a relentless, endless, shuddering wave. Your whole body screams 'flee!', but there is nowhere to run. Woe betide if you are caught in such a wind without shelter.

The winter wind that blew us off Mt Buller (1861m) in Victoria was not as fierce as a fully stoked New Zealand storm, but it recalled for me the same physical and mental anxiety of not knowing whether to stay in the shelter and risk being blown away inside it, or to get out and take one's chances exposed to the full brunt of the blizzard. Later reports spoke of gusts to 100 kph, which by New Zealand standards is barely a breeze. But our tiny bivvy tent was perched just a few yards below the summit on the exposed west ridge, and winds channeling up the northern gullies blasted the tent broad side, bending its poles and ruthlessly hammering our bodies braced against the tent wall. Needless to say, it ended our climbing ambitions for that trip at least.

---

[11] See Shaun Barnett, 'Rest in Peace, Angle Knob Hut', *Wilderness Magazine* (December 2011).

The full story goes back to 2021, the year I learned that there was winter ice to be climbed on Mt Buller's rugged south and western sides. The east side of Mt Buller is covered with easy angled ski slopes, and each winter attracts a delirious number of ski tourists who spend a lot of time riding around in lifts capable of moving 40,000 people per hour. The rarely seen south and especially western sides, however, are hung with steep bluffs, snowy gullies, and dark icy crags, and in the right conditions present diverse climbing challenges ranging from fifty degree neve-like snow ice or frozen grass to exposed, difficult mixed ice and verglassed rock, with short icy steps and the odd vertical waterfall up to sixty feet long. Protection can be laborious to find, and unreliable once you've found it, and one needs to be ready to use a mix of snow-stakes, ice-screws, pitons, cams, and nuts. Some of the best anchors are a slung icicle or a snow-stake hammered through the pack into the frozen grass beneath. A few permanent pegs can be found by scratching around under fresh snow. Once I even found a fixed rope buried beneath a frozen pack, set up, I suppose, to protect the dangerous traverse across exposed terrain at the base of the main western buttress. In all, it's like having a Scottish corrie just a few hours north of Melbourne, though, unlike Scotland, on my few ventures to Buller I have never seen anyone else climbing.

With climate change, good conditions for ice climbing at Mt Buller are apparently becoming scarcer. The area was first developed during the 1970s and 80s, and there are now named and graded lines of up to four pitches in length, along with an assortment of climbs that are too variable for any assignment of grade. The rock is terrible, and rockfall is a constant danger, especially once the sun warms the upper north and western slopes. The runout is also unforgiving, should you come off un-roped. Several people have plummeted to their deaths here, and not just skiers or ill-equipped hikers, having slipped from the icy west ridge below the summit.

The year 2021 was Victoria's second year of harsh lockdown in the name of COVID-19. I managed to get two trips in up to Buller with Arapiles climbing friend Ellen, once just before lockdown, once just after. Both times we hiked up from the Mt Buller village over the ski-fields, bivvying overnight on the west shoulder, then climbing up and down gullies and easy mixed ground on the southern slopes. Ellen had never been in crampons on snow and ice before, so we spent much of our time on the southern gullies rehearsing cramponing and ice axe self-arrest techniques. In 2022 I got in a solo trip quite early in the season, finding a thick snow pack and perfect freeze-thaw conditions. This time I traversed around to the western buttress routes, and was able to enjoy negotiating long runnels of ice before they petered out in steep and broken mixed ground, beyond which I was too chicken to venture without a rope. I didn't get as far around as the Waterfall Gully, which drains the big snow bowl on the north-western face. Conditions would probably have been perfect for it, but I resolved to return with a rope and climbing partner.

So in August 2022 Ellen and I teamed up again in the hopes that the big winter snows had had plenty of time to pack tight, and that the conditions would be right for an attempt on Waterfall Gully. We waited while a spell of clear and cold weather took hold, to make sure everything would be properly iced up, though by the time we were both free the clear spell was starting to tail off and the weather was looking like changing to a week of snowstorms, with gale winds in the offing. Undaunted, I had decided to bring my Black Diamond First Light tent, a superlight single skin bivvy that is supposed to handle fierce mountain storms but is not really made for sitting out inclement weather in. For a start, it's very tight for two, and once you're both in with boots, bags and gear, cooking inside is barely an option. The other thing is that its single skin is actually not that waterproof, and, while technically breathable, with two bodies inside and sub-zero temperatures outside, condensation soon accumulates in sufficient quantities to soak the interior contents.

It was mid-afternoon. We had caught the bus up from Melbourne via Mansfield, sparing us from all the kerfuffle involved in driving your own car. As we hiked up towards the summit from the village, dark clouds were building over the south and west. Pausing for a breather at the frozen Boggy Creek dam before heading up towards the summit, I wondered whether we were going to need the full two nights' worth of food and fuel we had packed. Perhaps we'd only get one morning of climbing in. The snow cover was superlative, the temperature nicely around freezing, but the barometer was steadily dropping. Hadn't I checked the forecast? What had given me the impression that the first front wasn't due till the day after tomorrow?

At the summit we stopped to put on crampons, before crossing the barrier that marks the end of the patrolled ski zone and the entry into dangerous territory. By now the wind was gusting and the odd shower of light sleety snow whipped across our hooded faces. The wind seemed to be coming from the west, and I guessed that it would swing southerly during the night as the building front approached. About 400 metres down the west ridge we found a likely spot to stamp out a tent platform in the snow. It was the same place I had pitched the tent just a few weeks earlier, but now the cornice had built up more and the lee side where the flatter ground lay had sunk and hardened. By using our ice axes we were able to cut blocks of snow out of the sloping ground and build a small wall on the western end of the platform to protect the tent.

The usual faff of erecting a tent in gusting wind was eased with Ellen's help; she held on to the tent corners while I crawled inside and fitted the poles to their lug ends and pushed the dome into being. We found rocks to anchor the corners, which I had extended with bungy cord for that purpose. I decided also to set out the guy ropes, which I hadn't needed on earlier trips, just to add to the tent's stability if the gale broke. With the crest of the corniced west ridge just beside it, the tent sat lengthwise on a west-east line, with the northern slopes dropping directly off to the broadside. If the wind stayed westerly, the tent presented only a narrow obstacle, and the little snow-blocked wall at its rear end would additionally aid its protection. If the wind turned south, I thought, we would at least enjoy the shelter of the corniced crest. For an hour or two we melted snow at the entrance and cooked up our freeze-dried meals. The space inside was so cramped we decided to keep our rucsacs stowed just outside, loading them with our boots, rope and hardware, then clipping them to the tent anchors so they wouldn't blow away. Darkness fell, and though the tent shook and rattled with every gust, everything felt secure and safely protected from the weather outside.

But about midnight the front broke and everything changed. Instead of turning to blow in from the south, the wind, now doubling in intensity, changed to a northerly. As the gusts grew in power, the tent, hit square broadside, was caving in. The two internal poles, which cross over at the roof's apex, were shifting, so that the tent's shape was losing integrity and threatening to collapse like an overstressed sail. To add to our concerns, the dry snow showers had turned to wind driven sleet, which with every gust sprayed through the tent wall in a myriad of tiny frozen droplets, filling the tent interior with a wet frozen cloud that settled on everything and began to soak. While Ellen sat up and leaned her back hard against the northern wall of the tent, I held on to the tent poles, trying to prevent them from shifting and bending out of line. For the first hour or so we managed okay, but instead of easing off, the storm grew in fury, and as the hours passed it was all Ellen could do to hold back the pummeling of the wind against her side of the tent. The roar inside was deafening, with verbal communication accordingly strained. Meanwhile we were becoming more and more soaked and chilled, with our sleeping bags and clothes half sodden, half frozen by the ice showers spraying incessantly over us. I also noticed with horror that the south side of the tent was beginning to cave in with a heavy drift of wind-blown snow that had been surreptitiously building up on the lee side. No amount of thumping against the bulging tent wall would clear it. We were gradually being crushed from both sides.

It was probably about then that the same feeling of anxiety began to well that I had experienced all those years before back at Mueller Hut in New Zealand: the question whether to fight or flee, to sit tight in the hope of a dawn reprieve, in the meantime risking getting blown away with the tent or having it ripped open, or else to make ready for an emergency exit from the tent and retreat through the storm to safety via the highly exposed and icy summit ridge. Around 4 a.m. I decided we had better get ourselves ready for the worst-case scenario, which meant we had to get our packs inside and packed, have boots and jackets on and our crampons and axes at the ready. The trouble was that neither of us could leave our respective command posts without risking the tent's sudden implosion. With some difficulty Ellen was able to keep her back pinned hard against the tent wall while taking over my firm grasp on the poles. Unzipping the front door, a slab of banked up snow collapsed inward, adding more slush to the now sodden interior. My headlight beam, scanning through the wind-driven sleet around the front of the tent entrance, revealed a remarkable sight: the rucsacs were buried beneath a thick sheet of rime-ice, as if protected by a shield. The guy ropes, also sleeved with rime-ice, now resembled stiff glassy ropes, over an inch and a half thick. The ice axes and crampons were nowhere to be seen.

I had to hammer my fist against the ice-shield to break the rucsacs free, and, having shaken off as much snow from them as I could, hauled them inside. While Ellen held the tent together, I first took out our boots, then began to stuff all our gear into the two packs - wet sleeping bags, stove, food, cooking gear and water bottles – and finally rolled up the foam sleeping mats and securing them to the packs. That gave us a bit of space to take turns in putting on overpants, pulling on our heavy climbing boots, followed at last by our waterproof jackets and gloves. We looked at each other by the light of our headlights and gave the thumbs up. We seemed good to go. It only remained to determine when, knowing that once out we had to move quickly but carefully to get off the exposed ridge and back down towards the village.

By now it appeared that the gusts were beginning to lessen in both severity and regularity. The jet blackness of the night had given way to a dark grey as the earth rolled slowly towards daylight. Now seemed as good a time as ever. We crawled out of the tent into the blunting teeth of the storm, and while Ellen scratched around to dig out the axes and crampons, bracing herself against the fiercer gusts, I began to unbury and break down the tent to stuff it directly into my pack. The frozen guy ropes gave me the most trouble, with the hard rime ice needing to be smashed off like sticky plastic against the rocks. As I took down the poles, the loose fabric of the tent ripped and jerked angrily against the rocks, so I had to lay my body down across the whole tent to untie the corners and release the tent for stowing. Once it was packed, we were able to get our crampons on, heave our packs onto our backs, grab our axes and pick our way gingerly back up the initially rocky west ridge, taking care not to trip or be blown off down the steep southern chutes yawning to our right.

At the summit, we could see well enough to turn off our headlights. It seemed odd to think we had been here just twelve hours earlier. Although the thick cloud and horizontal sleet hid the ski-fields from view, once we had found the still silent top station of the summit lift, navigation became straightforward, and we plodded down the slopes with the sleet whipping us on from behind. During the descent the sleet turned to rain, and when we reached the village, whose elevation lies some 1200 feet below the summit, the snow was turning to thick sludgy mush, and the village square was heaving with crowds of sodden, disappointed skiers and snow-tourists looking for some way to salvage their day. For us, similarly bedraggled, it was a no-brainer: call it quits and take an early bus back down to Mansfield. It looked unlikely that another coincidence of free time and freezing temperatures would open up for us that season. But now I know first-hand about Mt Buller's capacity to deal out a thrashing, I'll be a bit more careful to study the forecast.

Sunset from high on the west ridge of Mt Buller, 2022.

Looking up the western buttress of Mt Buller, with the line I soloed marked. I retreated at the steep icy step below the rock band near the top.

CHAPTER TWENTY-THREE
EPILOGUE

It feels odd having to write an epilogue. It seems like the end, but I know it is not. My dreams at night are filled with visions of mountains I am yet to explore, boundaries yet to be probed, climbing possibilities yet to be realized. Sometimes I get depressed at the increasing control and restrictions on access placed on great climbing crags and mountains all over the world. Last year, for example, I began investigating the possibility of heading to Argentina to attempt a solo ascent of the Polish Glacier Direct route on Aconcagua, the highest mountain in the Americas. Problem was, my naïve costings and plans were all based on my existing experience of climbing in Peru in the 1980s. It's not like that now. Mandatory permits and insurance; minimum party size; requisite employment of local logistical support; not to mention post-COVID international travel costs and reduced routing options: it all renders the goal inaccessible to me. I understand the rationale behind such controls, but the world has changed, and I am finding it hard to adjust.

Another potential climbing goal I recently investigated was to the eastern Himalaya in China. I got in touch with Japanese explorer Tamotsu Nakamura who has photographed and catalogued hundreds of unclimbed peaks between Lhasa and Chengdu, most of which don't appear on Chinese maps. Tamotsu's research, along with positive encouragement from an old contact of mine who works in a leprosy clinic in the Yunnan Province (yes, leprosy is still rife in many areas of the world), motivated me to start planning some sort of reconnaissance to the region, with one or two modest climbing objectives in view. But government controls and restrictions on access, all the more exacerbated in the post-COVID situation, make small-scale, freelance expeditions, just the sort I would want to organize, almost impossible to accomplish.

And so future chapters to this story are looking more and more likely to focus on relatively domestic forays in Australia and New Zealand. Having just bought a house in the Wimmera, Arapiles and the Grampians will surely feature front and centre (if National Parks Victoria don't shut down more cliffs). But it's the big mountains and alpine climbs that really stir my soul. New Zealand always beckons, especially winter climbs in the Remarkables and Darrans. But weather there is always fickle. My work commitments simply don't allow me the liberty I had in my youth to sit out long spells waiting for big fronts to pass. What about further afield? Could I ever save enough to travel to Norway and climb the giant Vettifossen? Or to Alaska to climb Mooses Tooth? Are such dreams far-fetched? Do my ambitions outweigh my abilities?

But you have to dream. For from dreams emerge plans, and from plans emerge real-life adventures. Health permitting, I have another twenty or more years of climbing ahead of me. But who knows what is around the corner? Who knows whether I can overcome the fears and doubts that continually plague me when I am actually on some cliff or ice fall, the fear of falling or breaking a leg, the fear of getting hit by rockfall, or worse than all, the fear of just giving up without having really tried. If intelligent failure is the key to self-knowledge and progress, then I don't mind "failing well" in my mountaineering career, nor do I worry about making only mediocre climbing accomplishments. What I fear is *settling* for mediocrity, for letting the ordinary define me, for allowing what is statistically average to limit my dreams and become the normal measure of my personal identity and worth, potential and destiny. That to me would be worse than death. Maybe I'll never live up to my own standards. I just pray I never abandon them.

Flowering cactus in the Santa Cruz Valley, Peru.

ACKNOWLEDGEMENTS

I would like to thank those who read earlier drafts or chapters of this book and offered both criticism and encouragement. They include Keith Lockwood, Jon Muir, Ellen Jalil, James Cooper, Simon Parsons, Val Pitkethly and Tim McCartney-Snape. My thanks also go to Tamotsu (Tom) Nakamura for encouraging me to publish an earlier digital version of the book in the Asian Alpine e-journal, of which he is the editor. I gratefully acknowledge the help of Peter King in digitalizing my old 35mm slides, and Ingram Spark for making possible the final production of this print version.

ABOUT THE AUTHOR

Adam G. Cooper is an Australian climber, writer, outdoor athlete, and academic. Born in Papua New Guinea and raised in East Africa, he has climbed on six continents over almost four decades. He has written numerous books and articles on religious studies, theology and outdoor adventure. This is his first climbing book.

www.ingramcontent.com/pod-product-compliance
Lightning Source LLC
Chambersburg PA
CBHW050312010526
44107CB00055B/2204